BLOCKCHAIN
UNCHAINED

The Illustrated Guide to Understanding Blockchain

PAUL A. TATRO

Printed in the United States of America
First Printing, 2018

Hardcover ISBN: 978-0-9980761-8-8
Paperback ISBN: 978-0-9980761-9-5

Published by Book Counselor, LLC
Bookcounselor.com

TABLE OF CONTENTS

TABLE OF FIGURES

CHAPTER 1
What is a Blockchain

It's hard to imagine that an 11-page white paper written by an anonymous author or authors could impact the technology world at almost the same level as the invention of the Internet. But that is what happened when, on October 31, 2008, a white paper entitled, *Bitcoin: A Peer-to-Peer Electronic Cash System* was published by an unknown using the nom de plume of Satoshi Nakamoto. The software built on the concepts described in the white paper was released as open source in 2009. Bitcoin became the first decentralized digital currency and spawned the new era for cryptocurrencies.

The digital currency world was not welcomed with open arms. Corporations, governments, and society in general disparaged Bitcoin and all its derivatives as a scam or a fad. It was the geek community that backed Bitcoin from the start and kept enough momentum going until, eventually, Bitcoin had a life of its own with no way to stop the movement. Bitcoin became the technological equivalent of a circus freak show. I remember a time when I walked into a county fair and was greeted by a tent that advertised, "See the World's Largest Horse - $0.35!" I indignantly said to my wife, "What idiot would pay $0.35 to look at a horse?" But, the seed had been planted and all I could think about was, "I wonder how big that horse is…?" Eventually, I spent over $10 bringing my family and friends in and out of that tent. Bitcoin became like that "World's Largest Horse." People scoffed, "So what, that never before in the history of the planet has the transfer of value between anonymous participants who don't know or trust each other been able to be validated and agreed upon through the use of advanced cryptography without the involvement of trusted third parties." Then people started to think… "I wonder how Bitcoin does it…?" When people began to look inside the Bitcoin tent, what they found was a concept called *Blockchain*. Ironically, the word Blockchain is never mentioned in Satoshi Nakamoto's white paper. While the many characteristics of what makes a Blockchain unique will be discussed later in this book, the key elements are encapsulated in the definition below:

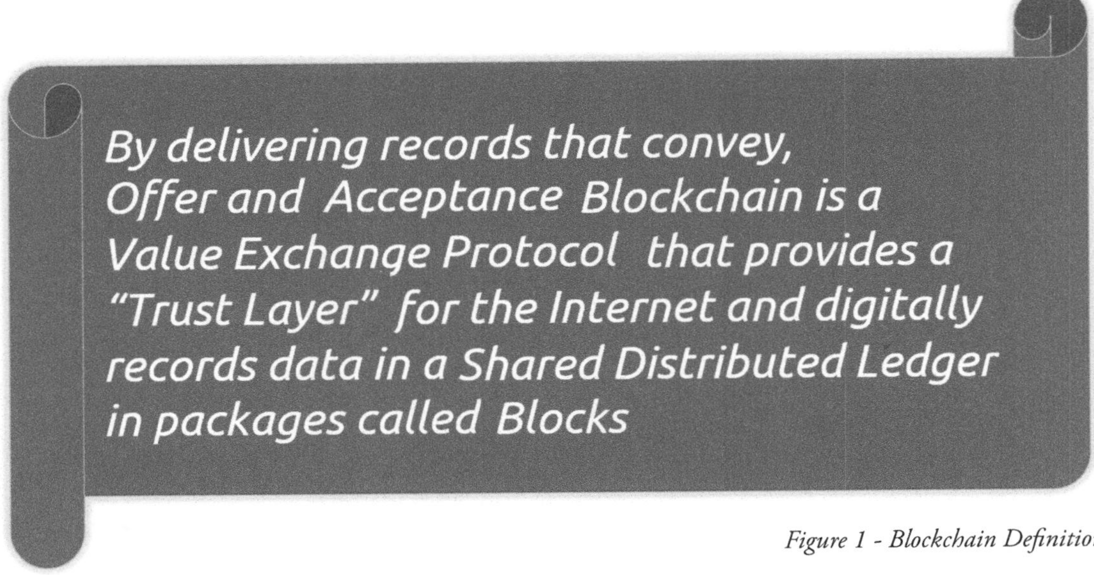

By delivering records that convey,
Offer and Acceptance Blockchain is a
Value Exchange Protocol that provides a
"Trust Layer" for the Internet and digitally
records data in a Shared Distributed Ledger
in packages called Blocks

Figure 1 - Blockchain Definition

DEFINITION

This definition has a couple of different layers as it moves from *what* a Blockchain is to *how* a Blockchain works. I want to pick out some key words from this definition that highlight the essence of a Blockchain. The first term is "offer and acceptance". Offer and acceptance is the fundamental component of every business transaction which speaks to the ubiquitous potential of a Blockchain. The next term I want to isolate is "value-exchange protocol." Creating transactions are one thing, but ensuring that the value and terms of that transaction are known and agreed upon without the need for an intermediary is, yet, another. The next term is "trust layer for the internet." Everyone knows the power of the Internet as well as the traps that are all over it. A technology that they can bring trust and assurance to the Internet is very powerful.

Now, the definition shifts from "what a Blockchain is" to "how a Blockchain works." The first term I want to isolate in the last part of the definition is "shared distributed ledger." The tedious back office job of accounting for and settling transactions becomes automated through Blockchain technology. This is a source of tremendous savings from a Blockchain and one of the key values that piqued the interest of corporations. Finally, the last term to look at is the term "block" itself. Blocks are the containers, or unit of storage, that hold the transaction history. Blockchains keep the provenance of all the assets involved in any transaction and once a block has been verified, it is very difficult, if not impossible, to make any changes to the data.

Having just defined what a Blockchain is, the typical reaction is "so what?" What problem does it really solve? To answer that question, let's take a look at a typical business scenario that does not use Blockchain technology and then we will introduce a Blockchain into the scenario and note the differences.

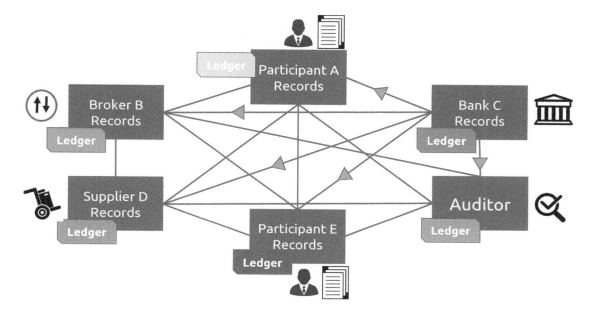

Figure 2 - Business Scenario without a Blockchain

The simple scenario above shows the usual players in most business transactions: brokers, suppliers, buyers, banks, and, eventually, auditors. Notice that each participant has a separate copy of their own ledger. When the interactions begin to occur, every participant has a system to keep track of who did what. Furthermore, there is no consistency as to *how* the various ledgers get updated as, undoubtedly, each participant uses different accounting rules when updating the ledger. Auditors are needed as the ultimate verification that the records are accurate, but auditors do not necessarily have a purview into all the participants ledgers. If something goes wrong it ripples throughout the whole network, causing every participant to revalidate their accounting of the interactions.

Now, let's bring in a blockchain. Below is the same business scenario with the same usual suspects, except this time, we've inserted a Blockchain in the middle of the transaction processing.

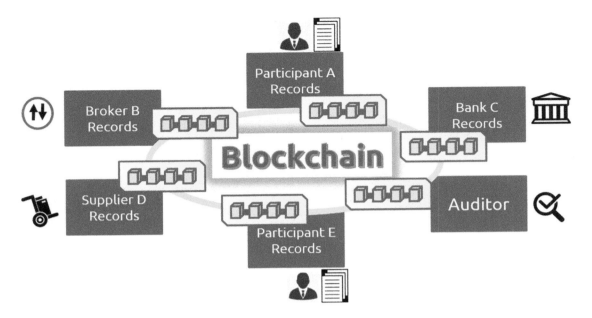

Figure 3 - Business Scenario with a Blockchain

Blockchains create a network that involves all the participants and acts as a verification mechanism for both transactions and asset ownership. A single copy of the transactions is stored in a shared, distributed, ledger that is replicated across the network so each participant has the exact same, accurate copy of the transaction activity in near real-time. The unique benefits that accrue from a Blockchain are:

1. **Consensus** – Consensus is a mechanism by which transactions are validated *by the Blockchain* (not by a trusted third party). There is a whole chapter of the book dedicated to this topic.

2. **Provenance** - Provenance is the capturing of the complete history of an asset. This history can contain quality assurance specifications or ownership history or anything else of value for a given asset.

3. **Immutability** – Blockchains are, for all practical purposes, unchangeable once a block has been added to the Blockchain. There is not an *Update* or *Delete* command in the Blockchain world as exists with databases.

4. **Trustless** - Blockchains operate in a "trustless" environment where the participants don't have to know or trust each other to participate in transactions.

Types of Blockchains

There are two types of Blockchains: public and private. Let's first examine the characteristics of a public Blockchain. Most likely, you have heard of Bitcoin and maybe Ethereum. Both of these and several others in the marketplace today operate using public Blockchains. Public blockchains are *permission-less* distributed ledgers. That means that ANYONE can join the network and you don't have to be asked nor do you need permission to join the network. Public Blockchains are *anonymous* so members don't have to reveal who they are to participate. Public blockchains also have *anonymous validation* which means that anyone can participate in the *Consensus* process that validates transactions. This opens the door for potential bad guys to try and tamper with the data in a Blockchain. This topic will be covered extensively later on. Public blockchains are *trustless*. Trust is not a prerequisite for doing business on the network. You do not have to know, or like, or trust the other party in a transaction on a public Blockchain. And, public blockchains are where the, what I like to call, "Brave New World" applications, are being developed. In other words, applications on a public Blockchain are the applications that didn't exist or *couldn't* have existed before Blockchains but are now being developed - like cryptocurrencies.

Now let's contrast public Blockchains with private Blockchains. There are several private Blockchains that are available on the marketplace. HyperLedger, which has big backing by IBM, and Ripple which focuses on high transaction throughput in the financial markets are two of the most well know private Blockchains. The first distinctive quality of a private Blockchain is that it is based on a *permissioned*, private ledger. Who can participate in the network and who can validate transactions is known and vetted in advance. Participants must have a level of *trust* within the network and be *invited* to join the network. Since private Blockchains usually have large corporations as participants, sensitive data will often be stored "off the chain" while consensus and validation information will be store inside the blockchain. For example, the fact that two companies agreed on a contract can be validated inside of the Blockchain, while the actual terms of the contract might be stored "off chain" in a relational database. Private Blockchains are the choice for "reconstructing existing world applications" where old applications get a facelift with Blockchain technology to gain the processing efficiencies that were discussed earlier.

Advantages of Blockchains

To summarize, a Blockchain provides for the highest degree of accountability in any application environment. A Blockchain guarantees the validity of transactions by recording it in several places. First, the transactions are stored in the main ledger. Then, the transactions are replicated across a distributed system of ledgers. All the network participants are connected through a secure validation mechanism so there is complete agreement on the value and terms of the transactions before the transactions are added to a block. The block data is complete, timely, accurate and widely available – this gives all participants a view of the data leading to complete transparency. Also, a Blockchain has *process integrity,* whereby transactions are executed exactly as the protocol commands, removing the need for a trusted third party. Therefore, there is no way to influence the blockchain process as there might be if you were dealing with a person acting as a trusted third party. It is virtually impossible to make changes to a blockchain after a block has been added. This *Immutability* comes from the fact that blocks can only be added (appended to the end of the Blockchain), not edited or deleted – all other databases allow for full data manipulation, but not a blockchain. A Blockchain is *resilient against hacker attacks* because decentralized networks have no single point of failure and are better able to withstand various types of malicious attacks. When the last two points are combined, Immutability and resistance to attacks, it yields the highest degree of data integrity.

CHAPTER 2
How does a Blockchain work

In chapter one, we threw around some big concepts like immutability, network replication, and creating a chain out of blocks of data. Defining these ideas is one thing, but demonstrating *how* these essentials are achieved, is another. This chapter is not for the faint-of-heart. We are going to go *inside* a blockchain to get a block-level view of how a Blockchain handles the addition of a new block and how a that Blockchain resists attempts to make illicit changes to data after a block has been added. So, zip up your wet suit because we're going in!

What is Hashing

Since a Blockchain uses advanced cryptography in the process of validating transactions, it is important to understand how hashing works. Let's start the discussion by examining what a hash is. A hash is a number generated from a string of text. This number is unique to the corresponding text string - *a "Digital Fingerprint"*, if you will. Take a look at the three examples below.

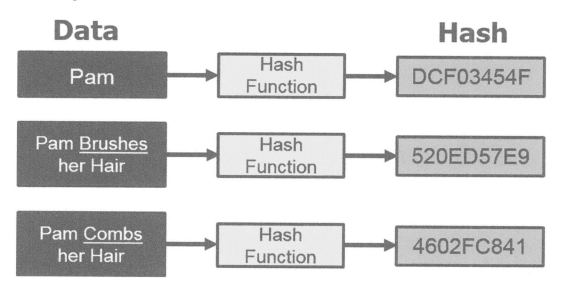

Figure 4 - Hashing Examples

Each of the strings of data, after being fed into the hash function, yields a random key result. In the majority of cases, the resulting hash is substantially smaller than the text itself. In our first example, where "Pam" was the only text hashed, then the resulting hash was larger than the text input. The other distinctive quality of a hash algorithm is that the resulting hash is always the same length regardless of the size of the text string that was input to the hashing function. In the case of a blockchain, the hash result is always 32 bytes. Even if you put all the text from the Library of Congress through the hash function, you would still get a 32-byte hash result! Hashes play a role in security systems where they're used to ensure that transmitted messages have not been altered. The sender generates a hash of the message, encrypts it, and sends the hash along with the message itself. The recipient then decrypts both the message and the hash, produces another hash from the received message using the same hash function, and compares the two hashes. If they're the same, there is an extremely high probability that the message was transmitted intact and without tampering.

Characteristics of a Hash

There are numerous hashing functions available. However, every hash, regardless of the actual algorithm used to generate it, has certain characteristics. For example, all hashes are *computationally efficient* in that it cannot take long to both calculate the hash or verify the hash is valid. Hashes are also *collision resistant* which means that they are generated using a formula in such a way that it is extremely unlikely that some other text will produce the same hash. A Hash should *hide information* about the input text string used to generate the hash. In other words, you should not be able to pick up characteristics of hashed info by noticing patterns in the hash result. Look at the second and third example in Figure 4 above. There is only one word different between the two text strings – Pam "brushes" versus "combs" her hair. Yet when you compare the hash results of the two text strings, there is no pattern between the resultant hashes. And, finally, hashed results should appear to be completely random. If you compared the resultant hashes of two strings that had a difference of one character, there would be no similarity between the hashes.

SHA 256

One of the hashing algorithms used by a blockchain is the SHA-256 (Secure Hash Algorithm) algorithm. While there are many different hashing functions used by Blockchains, we will refer to SHA-256 in the examples throughout this book. The general concepts are the same for the other hashing algorithms. The 256 refers to how many bits there will be in the generated hash output. Of course, the 256 bits yields a 32-byte (32 character) result. Remember, the hash is a digital fingerprint for the data. Here are some actual SHA-256 hash results when my last name, T-A-T-R-O is typed, one character at a time. Please take note of the resulting hash that is generated as each character is typed in:

The first hash is just for the letter T.

```
e632b7095b0bf32c260fa4c539e9fd7b852d0de454e9be26f24d0d6f91d069d3
```

The next hash is for the two letters, TA and so on.

```
518f962aec78efd4ff5a9268b7e03e5137736cf3d45dd38fca16cbfcde7d5f25
```

Finally, TATRO, looks like this:

```
cbc0fd36cc7da88c96cdd8d04f4131d3d45954766bdd063a69f36382f7ac2d17
```

Notice further that none of the hashes look anything like the prior hash and that there is no decipherable pattern to how the hash results. Also, if I typed my name in all over again, the exact same hashes that we saw as we went through the example, would appear again since these hashes uniquely identify the associated text string.

Blocks

Now that we have hashing under our belt, let's start our trek inside a Blockchain by looking at some of the information stored in a block. Please refer to Figure 5 below:

Figure 5 - Solved Hash

In this example block, there are four data fields as follows:

1. The block number – this is just a sequential number that gets incremented every time a new block is added to the Blockchain.

2. Nonce – is a number used in the mining process which will be explained in a few paragraphs.

3. Data area – This is the area that would hold transaction data captured in a block. In our example, it only holds some simple data.

4. Hash – this is the data field that contains the hashed output from the SHA-256D hashing algorithm for the data in the block. Think of the block number concatenated with the nonce, concatenated with the data area all being input to the SHA-256 algorithm as one string. The hash shown is the result.

Notice that the hash has the first 4 high order bytes of "0000". This is a special kind of hash that indicates that the block has gone through a Proof of Work problem solving process and produced a hash that was less than a system-generated difficulty value! Throughout this book, this special hash will be referred to as a "solved" hash. The number of high order zeros in a solved hash can vary based on the difficulty assigned to the hash problem, but a solved hash will have some number of high-order zeros.

In Figure 6 below, I typed "Tatro" in the data field, effectively changing the string of data that this block represents.

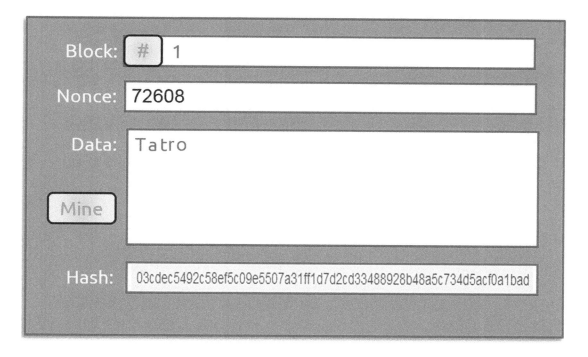

Figure 6 - Add TATRO to the block

So now, the data string that got fed into the SHA-256 hash algorithm contains the block number "1", the nonce of "72608" and the name "TATRO" (the string looks like this "172608TATRO") to generate a new hash. Notice that the new hash generated from the string that includes Tatro is no longer a solved hash! To bring this to your attention, the block color has changed to RED. Just as a note, the actual data that is fed into Proof of Work for a block is different than the data shown here but the general concept of how hashing works is the same.

How do we get back the solved hash? This is where the nonce comes into play. If I sat here and typed the number 1 [one] into the nonce field and calculated the hash and checked to see if the hash value was less than the difficulty target, then 2 [two], then 3 [three], and so on…I would eventually find a nonce value, that, when submitted in combination with the rest of the block data fields would yield a solved hash. And, since I don't want to manually iterate through that process, I press the "MINE" button in this example which will do this iterative process for me. Mining refers to the process of proposing valid blocks to the network which were provably difficult to create and is performed on each block of data in a Blockchain. This allows for achievement of *consensus* in an environment where neither party knows or trusts each other. See Figure 7 below to see what nonce the mining process finally discovered to generate a solved hash:

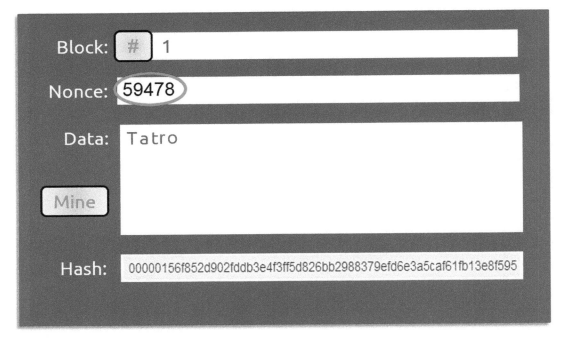

Figure 7 - TATRO with signed hash

To discover the new proof hash, the nonce number was incremented, combined with the rest of the Block data fields, and input to the hash function. If the hash result was not a solved hash, then the mining process continued to try new nonce values. The nonce that ultimately yielded a Proof hash is "59478"!

How do Blocks form a Blockchain?

As blocks get verified through the consensus process, they get added to the end of the Blockchain. Notice in Figure 8 below that a new field is revealed in the block configuration.

Figure 8 - Revealing the previous hash data field

The new data field revealed is the *previous hash* data element which is outlined in a red box above. The previous hash data field contains the proof hash of the previous block in the blockchain. This serves as the link that ties the blocks together in a historical sequence in the blockchain.

Consider the simple three-block blockchain shown in Figure 9 below:

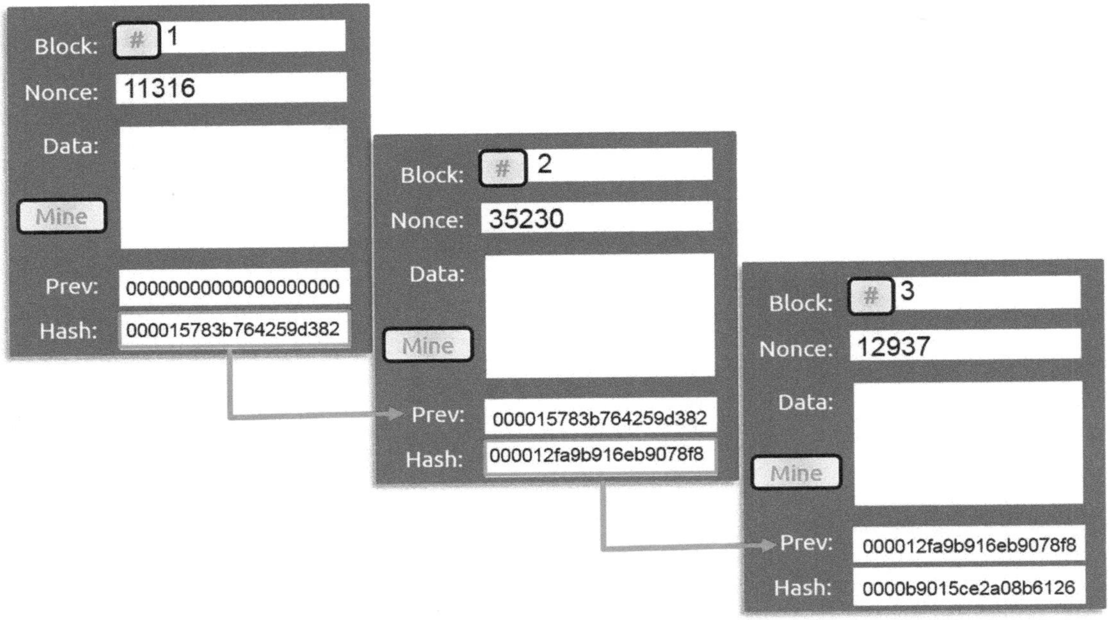

Figure 9 - Three-block Blockchain

First of all, notice that all the blocks have solved hashes in their hash data field, so immediately we know that these blocks have all been validated by the Blockchain. Next, note that hash of the previous block has been copied into the previous block data field of the next block, effectively chaining the blocks together to form the Blockchain. The last item to recognize is that the zeros in the previous of the first block indicates that this is the first block in the chain – also known as the "genesis block".

Attempting to Change a Blockchain

Now, take a look at Figure 10 below. Just as we observed previously, if "Hi" is typed into block 3, the solved hash gets broken – invalidating the block. Again, we highlight the broken hash by turning the block color red.

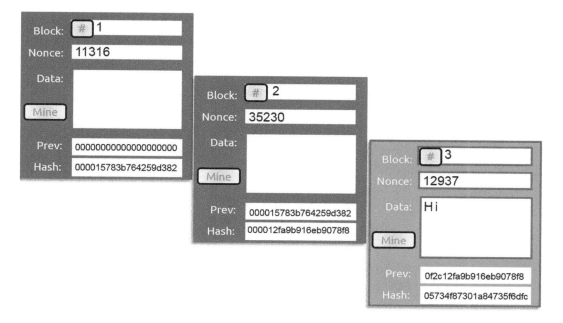

Figure 10 - Change to last block in a Blockchain

Now reset the Blockchain to its original state as shown in Figure 9. What do you think will happen if "Hi" is typed in the data field of the first block? Figure 11 below shows the result.

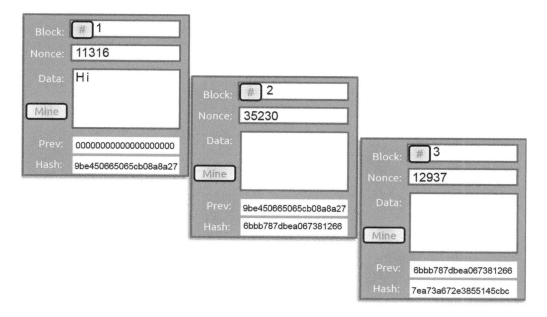

Figure 11 - Chain reaction of changing data further back in the Blockchain

15

Whoaa! What happened here? Changing that first block set off a chain-reaction (pun intended) across the entire Blockchain! Let's do a slow-motion replay and see, step by step how the Blockchain reacted to this change of data in the first block.

Step 1: *Typing "Hi" changes the data in the block causing the hash to be recalculated.*

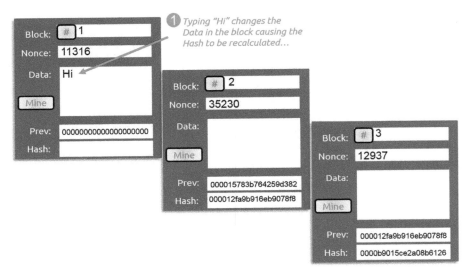

Figure 12 - Step 1, typing "Hi" causes block hash to be recalculated

Step 2: *The new hash is not a solved hash which invalidates the block. This is shown by the block turning red.*

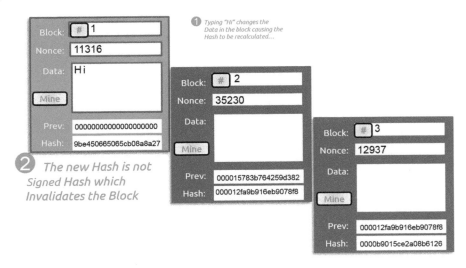

Figure 13 - Step 2, the new hash is not a solved hash

Step 3: The new hash that was calculated is updated in the previous field of the next block.

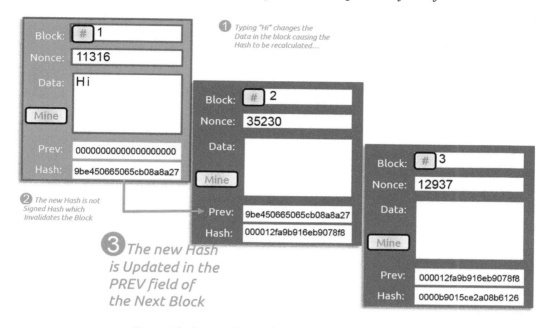

Figure 14 - Step 3, the new hash is updated in the previous hash field of the next block

Step 4: The change to the previous hash data field changes the data in block two causing the hash for the block 2 data to be recalculated.

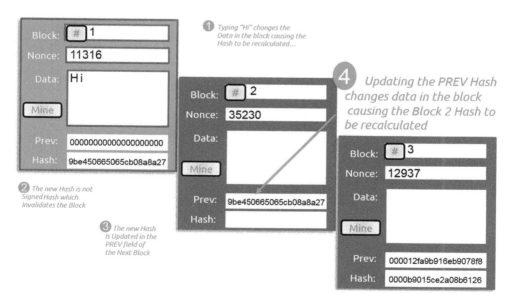

Figure 15 - Step 4 change to previous hash caused block 2 hash to be recalculated

Step 5: The new hash for block 2 is not a solved hash which invalidates the block.

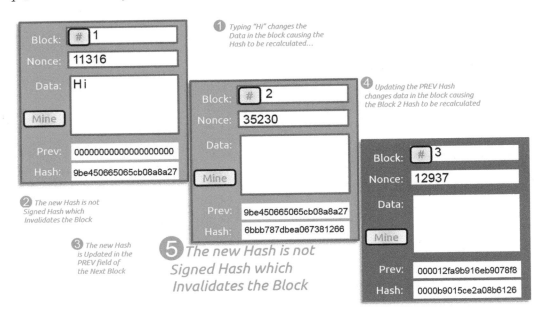

Figure 16 - The new block hash is not a solved hash, invalidating the block

Step 6: Repeat steps 3, 4, and 5 for block 3.

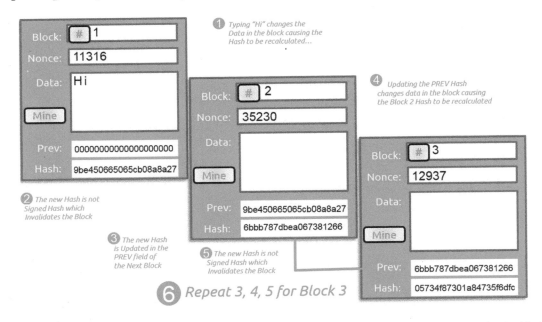

Figure 17 - Repeat steps 3, 4, and 5 for block 3

After seeing a step-by-step breakdown of how a Blockchain breaks or invalidates itself if any of the data elements are changed after the fact, what if a clever hacker wanted to change some values in a block to make it *look* valid across the entire blockchain? Let's see how this might be possible.

First, let's start with the final result of our prior example, shown in Figure 17. What if I go back into block 1 and mine for a new nonce to get a solved hash? The solved hash would propagate forward to the previous hash field of block 2 but would cause a new hash to be calculated in block 2. Notice that even though there is a solved hash coming from block 1, the new calculated hash for block 2 is not a solved hash.

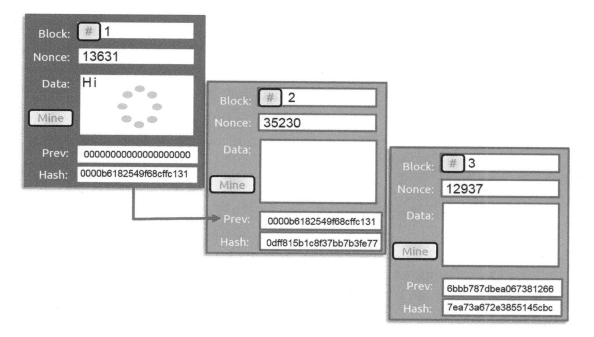

Figure 18 - Mine for a solved hash in block one

As is shown in Figure 19, the mining process could be repeated for blocks 2 and 3 so the blocks would all be signed and look valid again. Voila!

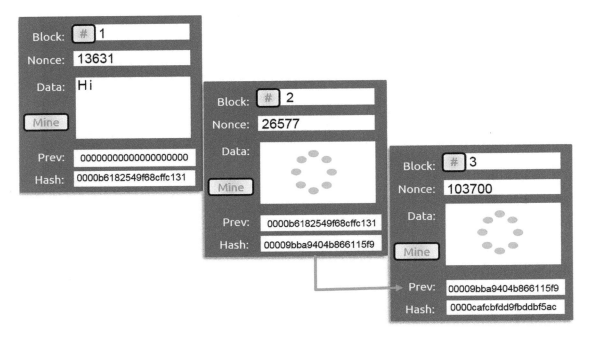

Figure 19 - Mine blocks 2 and 3 to make them look valid again

The further back in the Blockchain where someone might try to make a change, the harder and harder it is to get the follow-on chain to be good again. We saw in this simple three block example, how much work it was to try and make the blocks look valid again. This is how a Blockchain resists mutation and change. But, illicit changes were made to this Blockchain and we cleverly figured out a way to make them look valid. Is this a problem?

The Power of the Blockchain Network

How would anyone know if a Blockchain had been changed from its original values? This is where the distributed considerations for a Blockchain comes into play. Remember that a Blockchain is distributed across many peers in a network and that each peer gets a validated copy of the Blockchain. In Figure 20, the Peer 1 Blockchain looks exactly like the block chain from the prior slides. Peer 2 has an exact copy of the Blockchain and so does Peer 3.

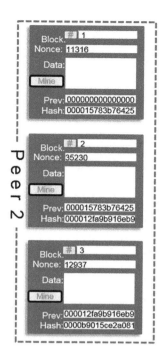

Figure 20 - Blockchain Distributed Network

Now imagine this exact same copy of the Blockchain across thousands of peers on the Internet, and they all have a complete copy of the chain.

We now know what would happen if "Hi" is typed into the data area of Block 3 of the second Peer. The block hash would become invalid. We also know that Block 3 of Peer 2 could be reminded to create a solved of work hash for the block. Figure 21, below, shows the new solved hash mined for Block 3 of Peer 2.

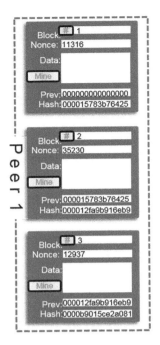 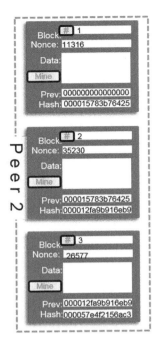 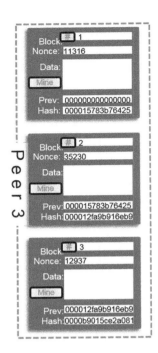

Figure 21 - New solved hash for block 3 of Peer 2

Even though you have all solved hashes, the two hashes in Peer 1 and Peer 3 are the same, the changed hash in Peer 2 is different. So even at a glance of this one hash, we know that something has changed in Peer 2! Even though it is a solved hash, it is different. It is different because it does not match the hash of block three in the other two Peers. Unless the Peer 2 node could mount a 51% attack (i.e., control more than half of the computing power of the combined network), the consensus of the peers will override the ill-intentions of a hacker.

Blockchains can grow to several hundred thousand blocks or more over time but rather than having to check all the blocks, you really only have to check the most recent block to know if something was tampered with. Notice that the more nodes that you have on the network, the more secure the network becomes because **the need for consensus among the peers makes unauthorized changes to the Blockchain nearly impossible to become validated!**

So, that is a Blockchain and a simplified overview of how the mechanics work. Of course, there is a lot more to understand about Blockchain technology, but this is a good start.

Tokens and the Merkle Tree

What has been demonstrated so far really doesn't appear useful since all we have been typing in the data area is "Hi" or my last name. The data area in a block is formatted to hold transaction data that has happened in the Blockchain. There can be several transactions in a given block. Here is where the immutability comes into play. If I change something in one of these transactions, it will recalculate the hash and initially, break the chain. Even if I remine that block, the hash will not match the hash of the other peer copies of the Blockchain. It is overly important with money and ownership that you don't lose track. So, a Blockchain's characteristic of resisting change is why they are useful for keeping track of asset ownership and other types of transactions in financial application.

Blocks can contain a variable number of transactions. In Figure 22 below, a new data field has been revealed in the block. The Merkle root is included in the block header. With this scheme, it is possible to securely verify that a transaction has been accepted by the network and get the number of confirmations by downloading just the tiny block header and the Merkle tree—downloading the entire block chain is unnecessary.

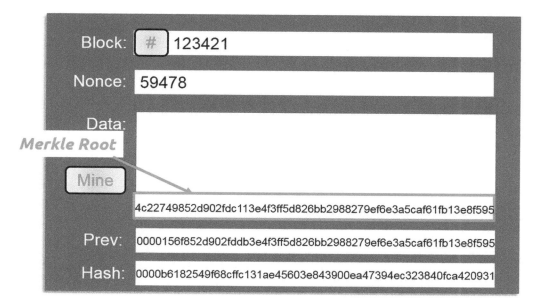

Figure 22 - Merkle Root

The Merkle root is the hash of all the hashes of all the transactions in the block. Easy to say but a bit more difficult to understand. To understand Merkle roots, you need to understand Merkle trees.

The Merkle tree concept was invented by a computer scientist named Ralph Merkle in 1979. It is widely used in cryptography but its most famous use is in Blockchain technology. In Figure 23, we will examine the mechanics of how a Merkle tree leads to a Merkle root.

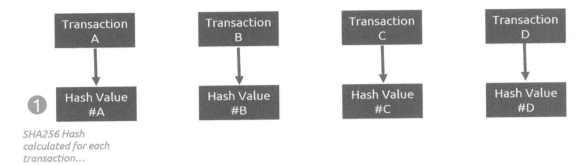

Figure 23 - Hashing transactions

In this simple example, there are four transactions referenced in a block. Usually, there are many more but this illustrates the concept. The first thing that happens is that **each transaction has a hash created for it.**

Then each pair of hashes are combined into a new hash. If there is an odd number of transactions, then the odd hash is combined with itself to so there is always hash pairs leading to the Merkle root.

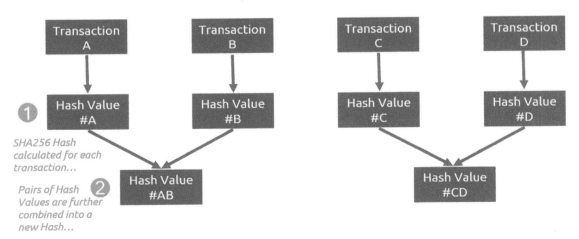

Figure 24 - Hashing transaction hash pairs

The final hash pair is combined to create the Merkle root.

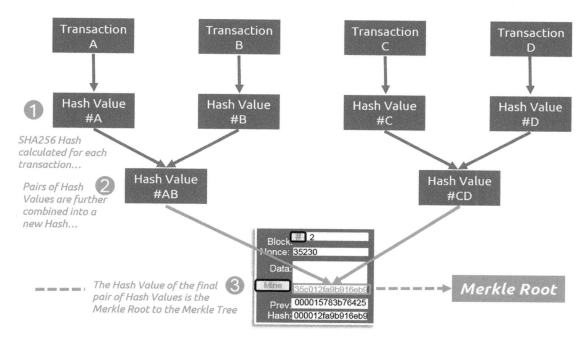

Figure 25 - Creating the Merkle root

Without the Merkle root in the block header, there would have no cryptographic proof of which transactions are included in a block, nor proof that their contents have not been tampered with.

Keep in mind that *transactions* are not stored in the Merkle tree, just the hash of the transactions. The Merkle tree stores the cryptographic proof of which transactions are in the block and the chronological order of the transactions. The Proof of Work that says, "this block is authentic" is based on hashing the Merkle tree input of all transactions. If a single detail in any of the transactions changes, so does the Merkle root. This includes any rearranging of the *order* of the transactions in the Block.

Finally, the Merkle tree gives several layers of check summing that are used to validate individual transactions, verify the tree, and verify the block.

This concludes Chapter Two. Let's move on to Chapter 3, Identity and Transactions.

Identity And Transactions

In Chapter 3, we will examine how a Blockchain knows the identity of who the participants are in a given transaction. We will also describe how identities are created and the relationship between public and private keys.

What is a Digital Signature

Let's start the discussion about digital signatures with a definition.

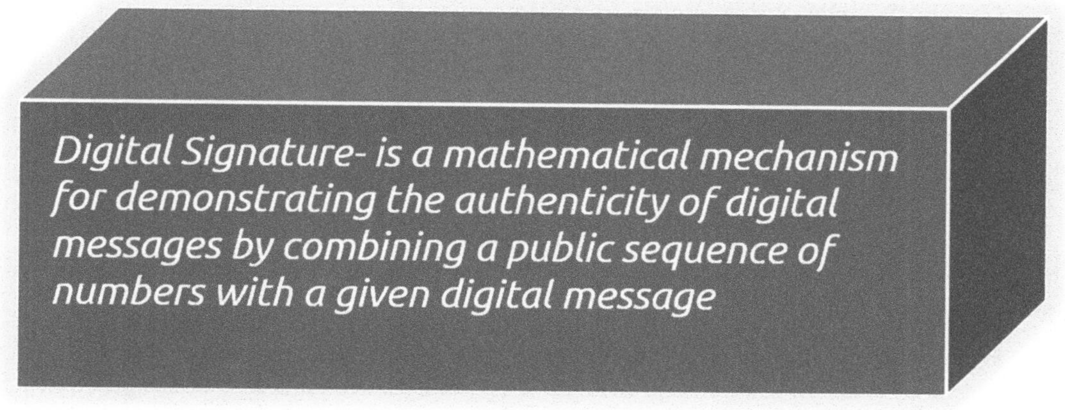

Digital Signature- is a mathematical mechanism for demonstrating the authenticity of digital messages by combining a public sequence of numbers with a given digital message

Figure 26 - Definition of a digital signature

Digital seals and signatures are equivalent to handwritten signatures and notary seals. However, digital signatures employ "asymmetric cryptography" to work properly. Asymmetric cryptography is also known as *public key* cryptography. Asymmetric cryptography uses public and private keys to encrypt and decrypt data. We will discuss public and private keys in more detail in a minute. These keys are simply large numbers that are related as the private key is used as input to generate the public key, but they are not identical, which is where the notion of asymmetric comes from.

One key in the pair can be shared with everyone and is called the *public key*. The public key is used to verify signatures of digital data. The other key in the pair is kept secret; it is called the *private key*. The private key is used to sign digital messages. We will look at an example to see how public and private keys are used later on in this chapter. The public key is used to encrypt a message; the private key associated with the public key used to encrypt the message is used for decryption. If an attempt to use any other key is made, the decryption will not work properly.

Digital Signature vs. Handwritten Signature

A signed paper document with your personal signature along with a seal from a notary is powerful identity verification, making it almost impossible to forge your signature. A digital signature is a mathematical way of providing the same assurance. But, what is the digital equivalent of the notary seal? Let's examine a digital signature scheme to find out.

There are several well-known digital signature schemes such as:

- RSA (Rivest-Shamir-Adleman) scheme
- DSS (Digital Signature Standard)

However, in every scheme, the user has two types of keys: a signature key (which is private) and a verification key (which is public). Take a look at Figure 27 below to see the process flow for how the keys are generated and then ultimately broadcasted to the Blockchain network.

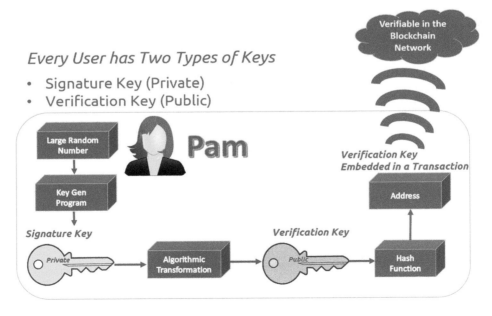

Figure 27 - Digital signature creation processing flow

The signature key is generated using a very large number which is fed through a key generation program and is used to mathematically derive the verification key. The verification key, along with information about the network and a checksum, is then transformed with a hash function to produce an address that other nodes on the network can see. You receive cryptocurrencies that others send to you with your address. As soon as any outgoing transaction is made which has the verification ("public") key embedded, the verification key is used to verify the user involved in the transaction. The verification key binds the user (Pam, in this example) to any messages that she creates using the signature key.

At this point, you may be asking yourself, "if a verification key is derived from a signature key, couldn't someone just create a reverse key generator that derives the signature key from verification key?" Cryptographers solved this issue by using a complicated mathematical algorithm to generate the signature keys; the algorithm makes it quite easy to generate verification keys from signature keys, but it is difficult to "reverse" the algorithm to accomplish the opposite. In fact, it would take the world's most powerful computer more than 40,000,000,000,000,000,000,000,000,000,000,000 *years* (that's 31 zeroes!) to complete this calculation.

Both the signature key and the verification key are large integer numbers, but since these numbers are so large, they are usually represented using a separate Wallet Import Format (WIF) consisting of letters and numbers as shown below:

5HueCGU8rMjxEXxiPUD5BDku4MkFqeZyd4dZ1jvhTVqvbTLvyTj

Now that we know how digital signatures are created, let's see how the digital signatures are used to verify transactions in a Blockchain.

Digital Signature Workflow

Let's examine how a message is processed and how digital signatures play a role in the process. Refer to Figure 28 below:

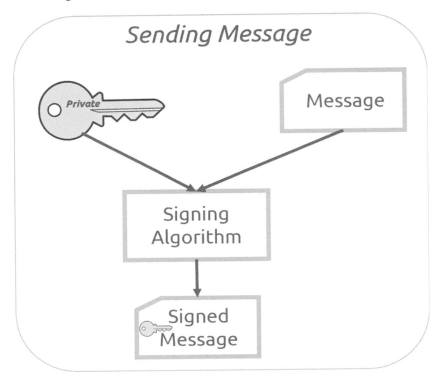

Figure 28 - Sending digital message process flow

On the senders' side of the message, the message to be sent along with the signature (private) key of the sender is input to a signing algorithm. The result is a signed message derived from the combination of the message and the signature key.

Figure 29 shows what happens on the receiving side of the message.

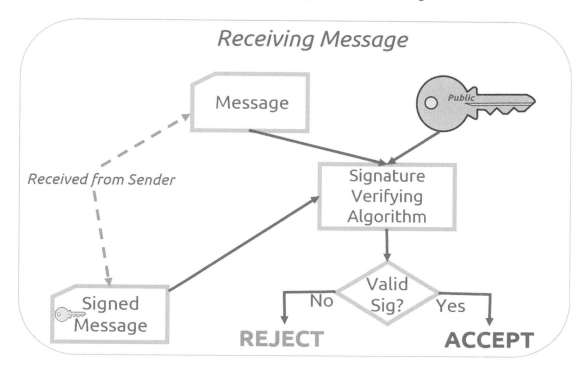

Figure 29 - Receiving digital message process flow

On the receiving side of the message, the signed message and the original message are sent from the sender. These are combined with the verification (public) key which was embedded in the transaction message when it was created. These three elements are input to the signature verification algorithm. The verification process only determines if the signed message is valid or not—it does not reveal the private signature key! So, if the message is determined to be valid, the message gets accepted. Otherwise, the message is rejected.

The private signature key is not needed for the verification process. The verification process is basically binding the individual whose verification key was used to *accept* the message *to* that message. This gives the digital analog to the traditional handwritten signature with a notary seal.

Digital Signature Benefits

Some of the benefits of digital signatures are the idea of combining the signature with the message itself and hashing the message before the process begins. By binding the signature key to the message, the message itself becomes part of the signature. This is very different from the traditional handwritten signature which never changes from document to document. Your signature is the same (or close to it) every time you write it and is in no way connected to the details of the document you are signing. With the digital signature, each message/signature pair is unique, which makes it even more difficult for forgeries to occur.

The message is always hashed before the signature is applied. Remember that the hash output is always 32 bytes which make the process easier for signing a message. By hashing the message first before applying the signature key, the programming process is simplified because programmers know that they will always have a fixed length 32-byte character string with which to work instead of a variable text string of an unknown length.

Blockchain Identity (BlockchainID)

A Blockchain identity (or Blockchain ID) is a generic term that refers to any identity on a Blockchain. Users can have as many Blockchain identities as they choose and can register these identities, just as one would register accounts on LinkedIn or Instagram or domain names on the Internet.

The main difference between Blockchain identities and accounts on any other service is that Blockchain-based systems have strong ownership. Blockchain identities can't be confiscated by any service because the system defines ownership according to ownership of public/private keypairs, just like ownership of coins on Bitcoin. This is in direct contrast to LinkedIn or Instagram usernames, which could be confiscated or censored at any time by their respective companies.

Sample Bitcoin Transaction

To see digital signatures working inside of an actual transaction, we will look inside of a Bitcoin transaction and note the role that digital signatures play. In this example, we have two participants, Pam and Bob. Pam wants to transfer 500 bitcoins to Bob (lucky Bob). Think of the transaction as a digitally signed declaration by one party, Pam in this example, to transfer bitcoin to another party, in this case, Bob. On both sides of the transaction you have both Pam and Bob's public and private keys. See Figure 30 above for a view of the transaction setup.

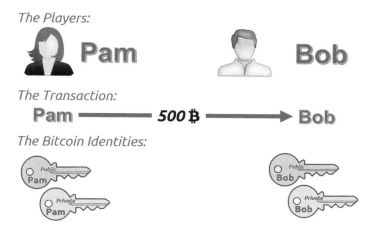

Figure 30 - Bitcoin transaction setup

Now that we know who is involved and what the desired result for the transaction is, let's look at the mechanics of how this would work.

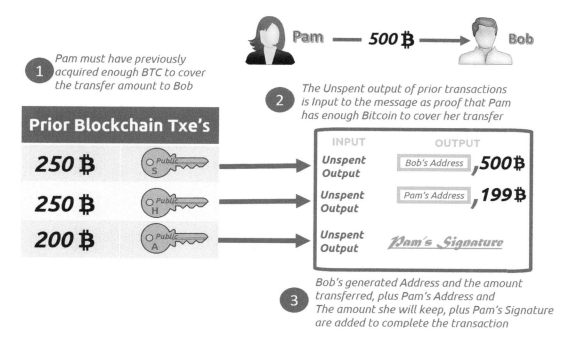

Figure 31 - Bitcoin transaction process flow

See Figure 31 above for the process flow of processing a Bitcoin transaction. The first step in the transaction is that Pam must have previously acquired enough bitcoins to cover the 500 that she wants to transfer to Bob. Notice in the Blockchain transaction table that Pam is receiving 700 bitcoins in total from three different people (identified by their verification key). So, clearly Pam has a big enough balance of bitcoin to cover the transfer of 500 bitcoins to Bob.

Step 2 in the process is to generate proof of Pam's unspent "output" of the previous transactions she wishes to spend now. The unspent output is then input to the message as proof that Pam has enough bitcoin to cover her transfer to Bob. In a Bitcoin transaction, the inputs must always equal the outputs that come from the transaction. So, in this example, since Pam had 700 bitcoins as input, there needs to be 700 bitcoins distributed in some way as output. The output side of the message shows Bob (who is identified by an address that was generated from his public verification key) getting a 500 bitcoins transfer from Pam. You never send bitcoin directly to a public key, but rather encumber the bitcoin in such a way that the public key related to the address you send the coins to is allowed to spend the coins and send them somewhere else at any point in the future. Also, 199 bitcoins are being transferred back to (or kept by) Pam. If you add 500 plus 199, you only get 699 bitcoins. We already know that the input must equal the output. There is one bitcoin is missing from the 700 bitcoins that we started with…this one "missing" bitcoin will be picked up by the miner that verifies this block as a transaction processing fee. Finally, to complete the transaction, Pam uses her private signature key to create a signature in the message hash which she includes in the transaction.

After the transaction is verified and packaged up with other transactions in a block, it is then broadcast to the other nodes on the blockchain network so everyone can update their copy of the Blockchain distributed ledger.

CHAPTER 4

Gaining Consensus

In this chapter, we will define "what is consensus?" and what considerations drive different consensus algorithms. Also, the original consensus algorithm, Proof of Work will be examined in detail. This single capability of consensus within a blockchain is the most powerful capability that it brings to the computing world. Never before in the history of computing has the transfer of value between anonymous participants been able to be validated and agreed upon through the use of advanced cryptography *without* the involvement of trusted third parties. The consensus mechanism built into a Blockchain effectively swaps politics for math in settling transactions.

Let's begin the discussion of consensus with a definition:

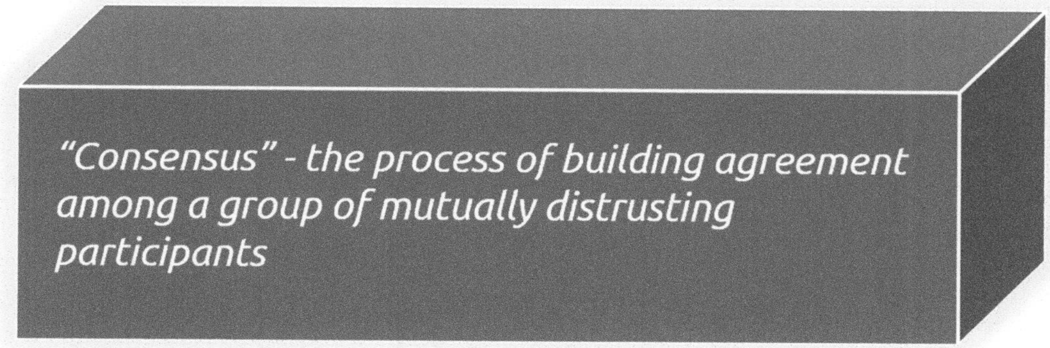

"Consensus" - the process of building agreement among a group of mutually distrusting participants

Figure 32 - Consensus definition

General Consensus Approaches

In general, algorithms for achieving consensus with arbitrary faults generally require some form of voting among a known set of participants. Two general approaches have been used with blockchain technology. The first approach, is "Byzantine fault tolerance" and the second approach is the approach often referred to as the "Nakamoto consensus" approach.

With "Byzantine fault tolerance" approach, multiple rounds of voting are required among participants until a certain percentage of acceptance is reached that the block is valid.

Nakamoto consensus is technically a form of practical Byzantine fault tolerance with some noted differences. With the Nakamoto consensus, a leader is elected through some form of "lottery". For example, with Bitcoin, the first participant to successfully solve a cryptographic puzzle wins the leader-election lottery. The leader then proposes a block that can be added to a chain of previously committed blocks. The elected leader broadcasts the new block to the rest of the participants who implicitly vote to accept the block by adding it to the end of accepted blocks on that chain. Regardless of which approach is used, all consensus algorithms have certain, common elements.

Elements of Consensus

When examining a consensus method, there are the four elements that must be considered:

1. Investment of the validator or miner (these are the nodes that process the consensus algorithm on behalf of the network)

2. Selection process of the Validator or Miner

3. Proof Element

4. Level of Trust

INVESTMENT - The first element is the level of investment needed to be made on the part of the miner or validator. What does the potential validator or miner have to invest in order to be able to process transactions and verity blocks? For example, if a Bitcoin Proof of Work approach is used to gain consensus (which we will look at in detail in a few pages), an up-front investment in specialized hardware needs to be made and an on-going investment of large amounts of electricity to work to solve a puzzle consisting of a mathematical function called a hash. This task is straightforward but extremely repetitive, and therefore computationally expensive. Computers compete to find a hash with specific properties. The miner that finds the answer first—the proof that they have done the necessary work—is allowed to add a new block of transactions to the Blockchain. Other consensus approaches, like Proof of Stake or even other Proof of Work implementations, don't put the same stress on processing resources or electricity consumption. And, since validators/miners must make an investment to participate, what incentive is needed to align the validators/miners self-interest with the best interest of the Blockchain network? Usually, there are both transaction fees or newly minted coins or both that incentivize validators/miners to behave honestly.

SELECTING THE LEADER - Next is the consideration of how the leader (validator/miner) will be selected from the pool of validator/miners? Most consensus methods involve some sort of lottery to randomly select the miner or validator that will put a block forward to ultimately be added to the Blockchain. Other consensus methods use raw elections and perform round robin selections of elected participants. There are several different approaches to consider and we will go through most these as we describe multiple consensus algorithms in more detail in a later chapters of the book.

PROOF ELEMENT - What proof element will be used? Figure 33 shows a partial list of the choices from which you can choose. New proofs are being introduced all the time, so this is a bit of a moving target. We will cover each of these in detail in the next chapter.

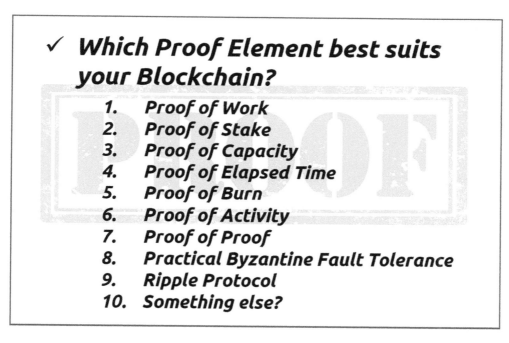

Figure 33 - Partial list of available proof elements

LEVEL OF TRUST - The last element is the amount of trust that will exist in your network. If you look at the Trust-O-Meter, you will notice that it shows a scale that runs between math and politics. In general, Blockchain replaces the politics involved with processing transactions with mathematics. Will the network be a completely trustless network as is the case in a public Blockchain? If so, you can rely only on mathematics to verify transactions. Figure 34 shows the Trust-O-Meter reading for a public Blockchain. Notice that the red ball is all the way over to the math side of the reading.

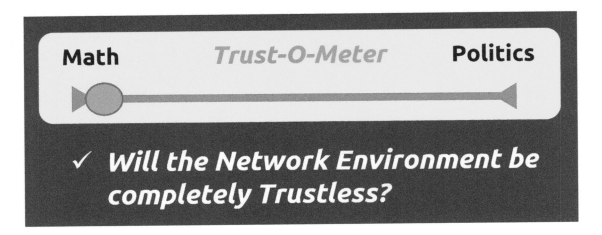

Figure 34 - Trust-O-Meter reading for a public Blockchain

On the other hand, if the network with be private, made up of trusted participants, then the Trust-O-Meter can scale back the processing required for all the math and rely, somewhat, on the trust built into the network. In that case, the red ball would be all the way over on the politics side of the Trust-O-Meter.

Objectives of Different Consensus Algorithms

Each of the different consensus methods has certain objectives that drive how the consensus algorithm will work and what resources will be consumed. There are four additional goals that a consensus algorithm will consider:

1. Performance
2. Scalability
3. Threat resistance against potential outside attacks
4. Failure model

PERFORMANCE - Certain applications that use a Blockchain will require faster throughput for higher volumes of transaction. For example, the Bitcoin Blockchain only processes six transactions per second which is too slow for high volume applications. Other Blockchains use different consensus algorithms to achieve better performance.

SCALABILITY - Next is scalability, which is the notion that, depending on the application, support for a higher number of concurrent users is a consideration for choosing a consensus algorithm.

THREAT RESISTANCE - Various threat models need to be considered in order for the Blockchain to be able to fend off an attack. If the attack cannot be completely prevented, the blockchain needs to make the cost of mounting an attack more expensive to attempt than the potential benefit of being an honest miner/validator of a Blockchain. For example, the proof of work protocol effectively protects the Blockchain environment from the "51% Attack". This is the notion that if a hacker could manage a processing power greater than 50% of the total processing power in the network, they could control who solves the math problem and introduce bogus blocks which could allow for double spending or other anomalies while they were in control. This is a *very* expensive proposition today in the Bitcoin environment and, for all practical purposes, is not possible.

The other example we mention here is the "Sybil Attack", wherein a trusted system is subverted by forging identities in the blockchain mining/validator pool. Again, this could give the hackers a tilted advantage of being selected to be the block validator and introduce bogus blocks to the Blockchain. There are several other attacks and more new ones every day, but thwarting these type of attacks is a consideration of each consensus algorithm.

FAILURE MODEL – Finally, since a Blockchain operates across a network, there is the possibility that nodes will fail as a normal consequence of network processing (and not due to an adversarial attack). The blockchain should be able to tolerate a certain number of these types of failures. With the practical Byzantine fault tolerance consensus algorithm, up to 33% of node failures can be tolerated while the system can continue to process blocks normally.

Now that we know the considerations and goals of the consensus algorithms, let's begin our detailed examination of the various approaches with a look at proof of work, which was the original consensus algorithm from the Satoshi Nakamoto white paper.

Proof of Work

Again, I like to start the discussion of topic with a definition. See Figure 35 below:

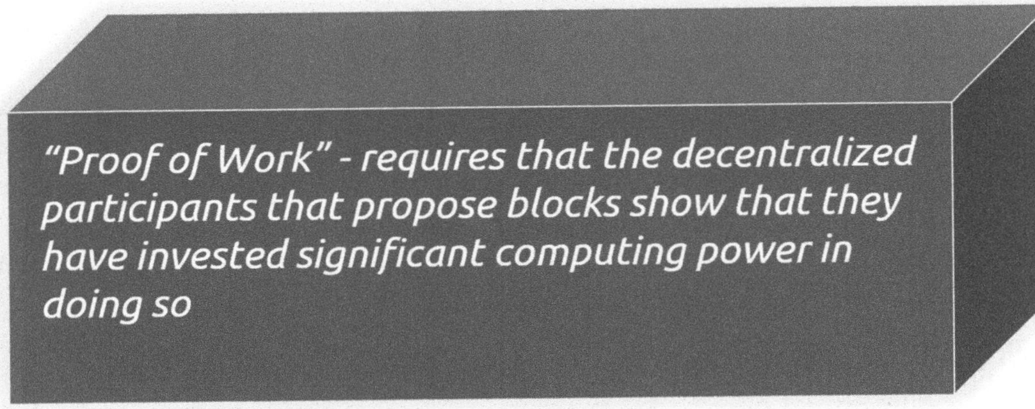

"Proof of Work" - requires that the decentralized participants that propose blocks show that they have invested significant computing power in doing so

Figure 35 - Proof of Work definition

Proof of Work requires that the decentralized participants that propose blocks show that they have invested significant computing power in doing so. You will recall that the concept of "mining" was introduced in Chapter 1 along with a discussion of a "nonce". Let's take a more detailed look at the mining process.

Mining Proof of Work

The first step in the mining process is to calculate the target hash. The target hash is influenced by the difficulty factor that is given by the system and used in the target hash calculation. The other input to the process of mining is the block header data which consists of the Merkle root, a timestamp, version, previous block hash, the nonce, and nBits difficulty, which is input to the SHA256D hash algorithm and a hash is generated.

These two hashes, the target hash and the hash output from SHA256D are then compared. See Figure 36 below and note the steps.

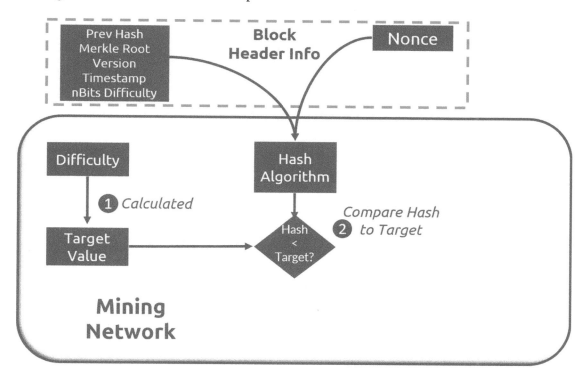

Figure 36 - Input to the proof of work mining process

Is the generated hash less than the target hash? If the answer is *no*, then the nonce is incremented by one and all the same data with the new nonce value is re-input into the hashing algorithm. This nonce incrementation and the regeneration of a new hash output continues in a loop as long as the resulting hash value is greater than the target hash value. Finally, some value of the nonce, in combination with the other block data will result in a hash value *less than* the target value at which time the Proof of Work puzzle is solved, and the miner earns the reward. Figure 37 shows the logic loop for comparing the SHA256 hash to the target hash.

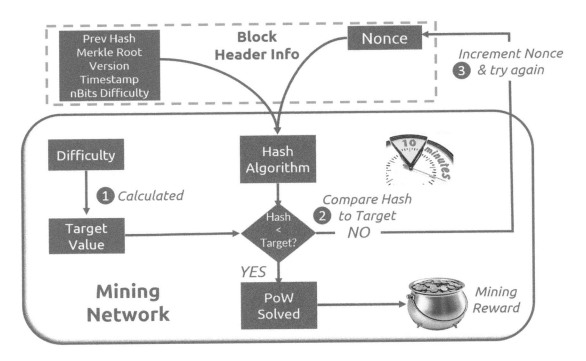

Figure 37 - Checking generated hash versus the target hash

For reasons of stability and low latency in transactions, the network tries to produce one block every ten minutes. So, every 2016 blocks (which should take two weeks if this ten-minute block production goal is kept perfectly), every Bitcoin client compares the actual time it took to generate these blocks with the two-week goal and modifies the difficulty target by the percentage difference. This makes the Proof of Work problem more difficult or less difficult. A single target adjustment never changes the target by more than a factor of four either up or down to prevent too large of a change in difficulty. This is an example of how the proof of work algorithm works for Bitcoin. Other Proof of Work blockchains have different parameters and different difficulty algorithms.

Proof of Work Workflow

As transactions are gathered into blocks on a Blockchain, the Proof of Work process flow is shown in Figure 38 below.

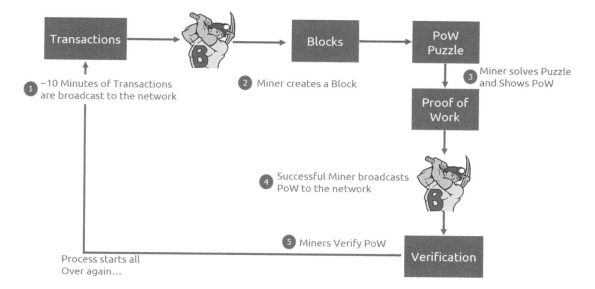

Figure 38 - Proof of work process flow

1. The first step happens approximately every 10 minutes, transactions that have been accumulated are broadcast to the network. This is not a sequential process in the sense that once a miner starts to process a block of transactions, every other miner waits out the 10 minutes for the next batch of transactions. There is an ever-changing *"mempool"* of transactions (and each node has a slightly different *mempool*), which is full of valid but unconfirmed (not yet put into a block) transactions. The miner takes the most profitable of these (which could include transactions from hours ago) which fit into the specified block size (1MB for Bitcoin, currently), and attempts to mine a block.

2. Next, a miner creates a block and begins to try and figure out the proof hash that will be less than the target hash.

3. Eventually, the miner mines the hash to solve the Proof of Work puzzle and shows the Proof of Work.

4. Step 4 is the successful miner broadcasts the Proof of Work to the entire network which includes other Miners and additional standard users.

5. In step 5, the miners verify the transaction and accept the proof-of-work by adding the block to the end of their copy of the Blockchain. Then the process starts all over again.

The example above showed how Proof of Work operates with Bitcoin. Other proof of work implementations allows for different parameters and, consequently perform differently.

Does Proof of Work really have anything to do with consensus?

For any distributed system to work, you must assume that at least half of the participants have good intentions. The problem is that you don't know who the bad guys are and who the good guys are. However, with a Blockchain, it doesn't matter, since there's no way of knowing who the successful miner will be, there's a greater than 50% chance that it is an honest participant. *But*, that's still not consensus. How does the network agree on valid transactions and blocks?

Let's look at an example of how the network nodes react as Blocks make their way through the Proof of Work validation process. See Figure 39 below for a look at how the consensus process works.

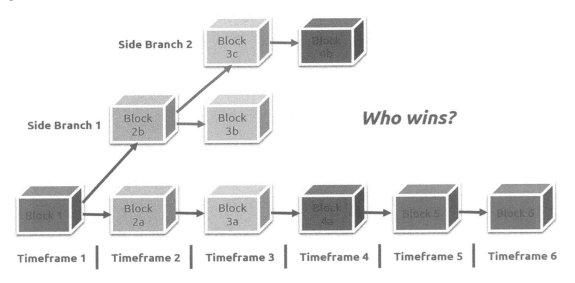

Figure 39 – Finding the Blockchain with the most consensus

First, we see that block 1 has been added to the Blockchain in the first timeframe. Next, block 2 is added to the blockchain but more than one miner solved the Proof of Work puzzle at roughly the same time. This causes a "Side Branch 1" to be created until it can be determined which miner's copy of the block will gain consensus. Notice, in timeframe 3, three blocks are added around the same time, causing a second Side Branch to be created. In the fourth timeframe, a new block is added to the original Blockchain and the second Side Branch. Finally, in timeframes 5 and 6, two new blocks are added to the original Blockchain extending it by six total Blocks. Which version of the Blockchain wins? Figure 40, below, illustrates how consensus would be determined in this example.

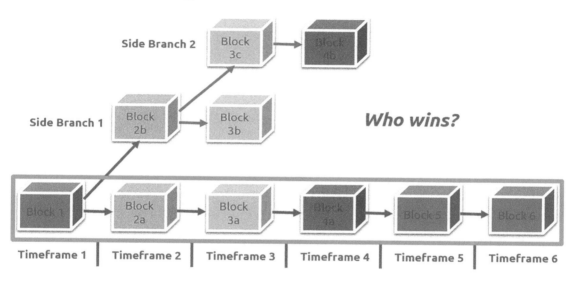

Figure 40 - Finding the Blockchain with the most Consensus

The Blockchain, or Side Branch, that has the most proof of work is always assumed to be the correct Blockchain! Basically, there are two possibilities that can happen when adding a block to a Blockchain:

1. The block further extends the Main Branch
2. The block extends a Side Branch and either:
    a. Does not add enough difficulty to make the Side Branch become the Main Branch.
    b. Extends the Side Branch with so much proof of work to make it become the new Main Branch.

The bottom line is that consensus goes to the branch that has the most work put into it.

This concludes our review of consensus and the Proof of Work consensus algorithm. In Chapter 5, we will dive into the details of the practical Byzantine fault tolerance and Proof of Stake consensus algorithms.

CHAPTER 5
Practical Byzantine Fault Tolerance & Proof Of Stake

Having just finished examining the concepts behind consensus and looking into the details of how Proof of Work operates, Chapter 5 will detail the practical Byzantine fault tolerance consensus method and a popular derivative, the Ripple protocol. We will also break down Proof of Stake and contrast it with Proof of Work to see the trade-offs between the two.

The beauty of Blockchain technology is that it replaces politics with math. And, according to George Polya, a famous mathematician from Stanford, mathematics is the cheapest science because all you need is a pencil and paper. Of course, that quote was made before advanced cryptography was needed to solve repetitive math puzzles in a Proof of Work scenario. To solve these puzzles takes a special type of chip, called an ASIC (Application Specific Integrated Circuit) which is designed to perform SHA-256 hash algorithms at very high speeds. The current capacity of the combined Bitcoin miners as of October of 2016 is approximately 3.75 million tera-hashes per second and growing. To provide that hashing power takes a lot of investment in specialized ASICs as well as consuming a large amount of electricity.

According to the Bitcoin Energy Consumption Index as of October of 2016, Bitcoin mining is pegged at an estimated annual electricity consumption value of 14.54 terawatt hours (TWh). That means that the average Bitcoin transaction requires 163 kilowatt hours (KWh) of electricity, which is enough to power the average U.S. household for about five and a half days. That would also put Bitcoin on par with Turkmenistan, which ranks 81st when it comes to the energy consumption rankings of countries around the globe. Read more at https://hotardware.com/news/ethereum-and-bitcoin-energy-consumption-surpass-entire-countries-power-budgets#OYUxih12izXScRA0.99. The cost of ASICs and the energy consumption requirements to run them are a couple of the main contributing factors to why alternative consensus methods to Proof of Work have been developed.

Perceived issues with Proof of Work

As we learned in Chapter 4, Proof of Work is very mathematically intensive because of the iterative generations of hashes after incrementing a nonce to try and find a hash output smaller than the target value generated by the system. Criticisms of this approach are:

1. This requires a constant, ongoing expenditure of resources, for the system to just work normally.

2. Solving the Proof of Work puzzle adds to the processing time of every transaction. You'll remember that the system tries to keep the block processing time right at ten minutes.

3. The work must be done regardless of whether someone is trying to interfere or not. Proof of Work is not executed in response to an attack of some kind; it is executed for every block.

4. Someone has to pay the miners for their work. Miner compensation comes in the form of transaction fees and newly minted coins.

5. The miner salary must be doled out whether or not anyone is attacking the Blockchain, which seems inefficient.

These are the perceived issues with Proof of Work. I will qualify that these are issues perceived with the Proof of Work algorithm as implemented in Bitcoin. Many other networks (like Ethereum) currently employ a Proof of Work hashing algorithm that can be done with consumer CPUs, GPUs, and FPGAs so they consume far less resources. So, even though the Proof of Work consensus method has led to the *never-before-in-the history-of-computing* capability to verify anonymous transactions between parties that don't trust each other, Proof of Work may well become "Poof of Work" and disappear from Blockchain processing as alternatives are constantly being developed. Let's look at one of the alternative consensus approaches, the practical Byzantine fault tolerance consensus algorithm.

The Byzantine General's Problem

Practical Byzantine fault tolerance consensus is an approach to solving the Byzantine Generals' Problem. With the Byzantine Generals' problem, a group of generals, each commanding a portion of the Byzantine army, encircle a city. In Figure 41 below, you can see that the generals have encircled a castle, and more specifically, a white castle! These

Generals wish to formulate a plan for attacking the city. In its simplest form, the generals must only decide whether to attack or retreat. Some generals may prefer to attack, while others prefer to retreat. The most important element is that every general act in unison, because a misinformed attack by a few generals would become a disaster and end up being worse than a coordinated attack or a coordinated retreat.

- Generals of Army surround Enemy City
- Action in Unison required to win
- Some Generals may be Traitors
  - ✓ Prevents loyal Generals from reaching agreement
  - ✓ Sabotages collective action
  - ✓ Fail to act
- Distributed Systems must cope with the failure/sabotage of its constituents

Figure 41 - The Byzantine Generals' Problem

The problem is complicated further by the fact that some generals may be traitors who may cast a vote for a suboptimal strategy. Or, the traitors may vote one way when communicating with some of the generals and the opposite way when communicating with others. For instance, if nine generals are voting, four of whom support attacking while four others are in favor of retreat, the ninth general may send a vote of retreat to those generals in favor of retreat, and a vote of attack to the rest. Those who received a retreat vote from the ninth general will retreat, while the rest will attack (which will not go well for the attackers). The problem is complicated further by the fact that the generals are geographically separated and have to send their votes via messengers. The messengers could add additional complications in that they may fail to deliver the votes or may forge false votes.

To map the Byzantine Generals' Problem to a Blockchain network computing world, the "generals" in the example are the nodes participating in the distributed Blockchain network. The messengers are the communication links across the Blockchain network. The collective goal of the "loyal generals" is to decide whether or not to accept a transaction submitted to the Blockchain as being valid or not and to extend the Blockchain with valid blocks. Loyal generals are interested in ensuring the integrity of the Blockchain and therefore ensuring that only correct information is accepted. The deceitful generals, on the other hand, would be any party seeking to falsify information on the Blockchain. So, the system has to deal with unexpected node failures (dishonest messengers or messengers who didn't make it to deliver the message) and the possible direct sabotage of its constituents which are like deceitful generals.

Practical Byzantine Fault Tolerance Consensus Method

Practical Byzantine fault tolerance is alternative to Proof of Work consensus. The practical Byzantine fault tolerance algorithm guarantees that all honest nodes in the network decide upon the same plan of action, even though a small number of deceitful nodes may be present. Practical Byzantine fault tolerance protects against various threats such as the arbitrary concurrent node failure (a Byzantine fault) of multiple network nodes or deceitful behavior on the part of dishonest nodes. Using this approach, a Blockchain network of (N) nodes can withstand the failure (either through deceit or node failure) of (f) number of Byzantine nodes, where f = (N-1)/3. Or, stated another way, practical Byzantine fault tolerance can withstand the failure of 33% of the nodes and still function effectively. The reverse view of the formula above is that the algorithm ensures that a minimum of 67% of the nodes reach consensus on the validity and order of transactions before appending them to the shared ledger. Figure 42 below shows the processing flow of a Blockchain using practical Byzantine fault tolerance as its consensus method.

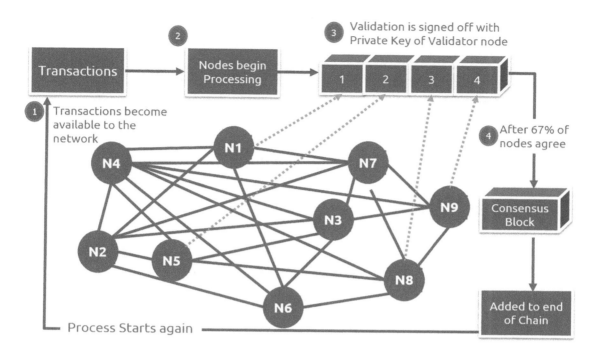

Figure 42 - Practical Byzantine fault tolerance process flow

1. First, transactions become available for processing.

2. The nodes begin putting the transactions through the validation process.

3. The red dashed lines show that as each node completes their validation process, a format that is signed with the node's private key is returned, signaling that particular nodes acceptance of the Block of transactions.

4. Once enough identical responses are collected (this would be 67% of the nodes), a consensus block is built and added to the end of the Blockchain. Then the process begins all over again.

There is more than one approach to the practical Byzantine fault tolerance consensus method. Let's take a look at the Ripple protocol consensus algorithm and see how it is different.

Ripple Protocol Consensus Method

The Ripple protocol offers an alternative form of practical Byzantine fault tolerance consensus method. The Ripple protocol was developed by Ripple Labs with the specific task of moving money and payments around the world as frictionless and quickly as possible. Ripple Labs wanted to come up with a faster and more efficient mechanism than Proof of Work, so some of their objectives included:

- Reduce Latency - By utilizing *"collectively-trusted subnetworks"* called Unique Node Lists, Ripple could shorten the time it takes to reach consensus. Recall that in Chapter 4, the various trade-offs and considerations when establishing a consensus method were listed. The Ripple protocol is an example of tweaking practical Byzantine fault tolerance specifically for a payment system to improve the throughput of processing transactions.

- Overcome the three main challenges that distributed payment systems face:
  1. Correctness – discerning between correct and fraudulent transactions without consulting a trusted third party.
  2. Agreement – maintain a single, global truth captured in a blockchain.

Utility – improve the overall latency of the system so transactions could be processed in a matter of seconds instead of waiting the several days that it takes to transfer money with predecessor systems.

Unique Node Lists

One of the key differences between practical Byzantine fault tolerance and the Ripple protocol is the idea of a Unique Node List (UNL). With the Ripple protocol, nodes are grouped into Unique Node Lists. Figure 43 below shows how the Ripple protocol takes the group of Validator nodes and breaks them into UNLs.

Shortening the Consensus Process

Entire Network

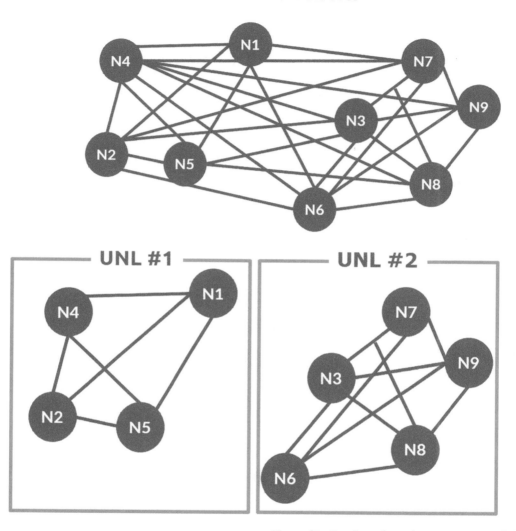

Figure 43 - Breaking the nodes into unique node lists

Unique Node Lists have the following characteristics:

1. Each server maintains its own Unique Node List.

2. *Only* the votes of other members of the Unique Node List are considered for consensus. This is a very critical point. By reducing the number of nodes that need to perform consensus, the time it takes to verify transactions is reduced!

3. Nodes can belong to more than one Unique Node List. So if we added a third UNL to our example, nodes 1 and 7 *could* be participants in that UNL as well.

4. Of course, the constituents that make up the Unique Node List are trusted not to collude to defraud the network

Ripple Protocol Process Flow

Refer to figure 44 below for the steps involved with the Ripple protocol consensus algorithm.

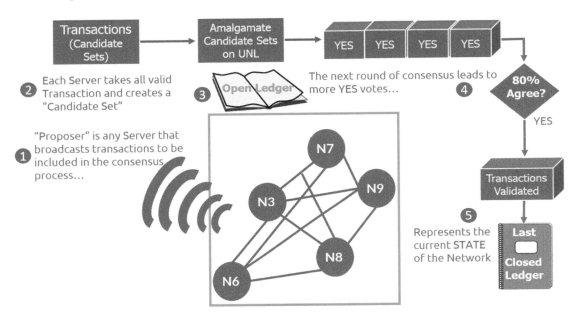

Figure 44 - Ripple protocol consensus algorithm process flow

1. Step one, one of the Unique Node Lists, UNL #2 in this example, becomes a "proposer" by broadcasting the transactions to be included in the consensus process to the network.

2. Next, each server takes all the valid transactions and creates a "candidate set" for processing.

3. The candidate sets are combined on the proposer's Unique Node List. During the time that the transactions are being processed for consensus, the proposer's UNL ledger is considered to be "OPEN".

4. The nodes inside the proposer's Unique Node List validate the transaction and register their vote on the validity of the candidate set. If the necessary number of

votes has not been reached, then additional rounds of voting are undertaken until the minimum number of votes required for consensus is gained. In the case of the Ripple protocol, 80% of the UNL must validate the transaction for consensus to be reached. If 80% of the nodes have not validated the candidate set, then another round of voting is required. Eventually, the 80% threshold is crossed, and the candidate set of transactions are validated in the open ledger.

5. The ledger of the UNL that had been "opened" at the beginning of this process is now "Closed". The last closed ledger in the Ripple network is considered to be the current state of the Blockchain. Some view the Ripple protocol as being based on *Proof of Authority* as specific nodes (the nodes that are members of the Unique Node List) are given the authority to validate transactions. Notice that the Ripple protocol does not save the transactions into blocks but uses the last closed ledger as the current state of the Blockchain. For this reason, Ripple isn't considered to be a Blockchain by some.

Practical Byzantine fault tolerance and the Ripple protocol were two examples of consensus following an approach that solves the Byzantine Generals' problem. Next, we will look Proof of Stake.

Proof of Stake

See Figure 45 for the definition of Proof of Stake.

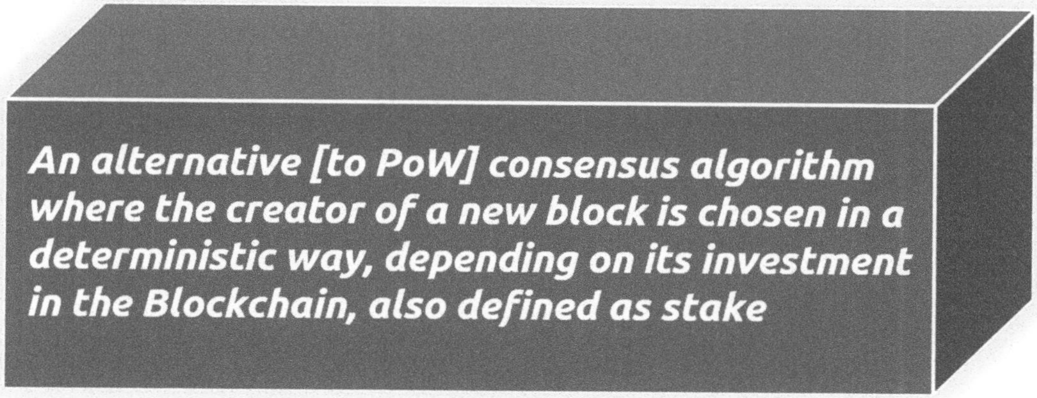

An alternative [to PoW] consensus algorithm where the creator of a new block is chosen in a deterministic way, depending on its investment in the Blockchain, also defined as stake

Figure 45 - Proof of Stake definition

Proof of Stake is *an alternative to the Proof of Work consensus algorithm where the creator of a new block is chosen in a deterministic way, depending on the creators' wealth or investment in the Blockchain, also defined as stake.* Proof of Stake is really a category of many closely-related consensus protocols, and several of the variations will be looked at in detail late on this book. As we will see, Proof of Stake aligns the validators' objectives to ensure transaction integrity by requiring that all validators have invested in the Blockchain in which they operate. Some examples of Blockchains that use the Proof of Stake consensus algorithm are: Peercoin, Neucoin, Blackcoin, Mint Coin, OK Cash, Red Coin, and Diamond Coin.

Differences between Proof of Stake and Proof of Work

As Proof Stake and Proof of Work are two of the most popular consensus methods, it is important to do a point by point comparison and note the fundamental differences between the two approaches. See Figure 46 below for a succinct comparison.

Proof of Work	Proof of Stake
1. Capital invested in Hardware and Power	1. Capital invested in local Coins and placed in PoS Mechanism
2. "Miners" solve Puzzles to secure transactions	2. "Validators" create next block on the chain
3. 1st Miner to solve Puzzle wins reward	3. Validator selected from a pool based on a weighted, random selection algorithm
4. Tremendous amounts of power consumed	4. A fraction of the power consumed by PoW

Figure 46 - Comparison of Proof of Work and Proof of Stake

1. The first category of comparison is what capital investment must be made to validate blocks? How much of an investment do miners and validators have to spend to participate as a miner in Proof of Work and a Validator in Proof of Stake? With Proof of Work as we saw with the Bitcoin example in Chapter 4,

a large investment is made in both the computer hardware to perform all the hashing and the electrical power to run this equipment. Some estimate that over $400 million per year is spent just on electricity in the Bitcoin mining network alone. On the other hand, the investment a Proof of Stake validator makes is in the local coins of their Blockchain and into the Proof of Stake mechanism itself.

2. The next consideration is "Who does the Work?" With Proof of Work, you have "miners" who solve complex mathematical puzzles and with Proof of Stake and you have "validators" who authenticate the blocks that are added to the Blockchain. Actually, some of the earliest implementations of Proof of Stake (like with Peercoin and Neucoin) referred to Proof of Stake miners. The notion of validators has come into the market more recently.

3. How are the miners and validators selected? We learned in Chapter 3 that there is usually some form of random selection process as part of the consensus method. With Proof of Work, the first miner to solve the math puzzle is the one selected to add the block to the Blockchain. With Proof of Stake, in general, the validator is selected based on a weighted, random selection algorithm. The weighted portion of the selection comes from the amount of investment the validator has in the local coins – the more coins you have invested, the more weight you have in the selection process. Across the different versions of Proof of Stake there are a variety of different metrics to determine the "weight" of a particular "validator"/ miner. The original Peercoin Proof of Stake implementation used something called, stake weight, which was a combination of the number of coins invested (stake) multiplied by the time that had passed since you last spent any coins. So, if you had five coins that hadn't been moved for 30 days, you had 150 coinage or stake weight.

4. The final category for comparison is how much resource is consumed to carry out the consensus method? Here it comes down to power consumption. With Proof of Work, a tremendous amount of power is consumed in comparison to Proof of Stake which only consumes a fraction of the power.

So, you can see that there are some stark differences between Proof of Work and Proof of Stake. Now let's examine the process flow of Proof of Stake.

Proof of Stake Process Flow

Refer to Figure 47 below that depicts the Proof of Stake process flow.

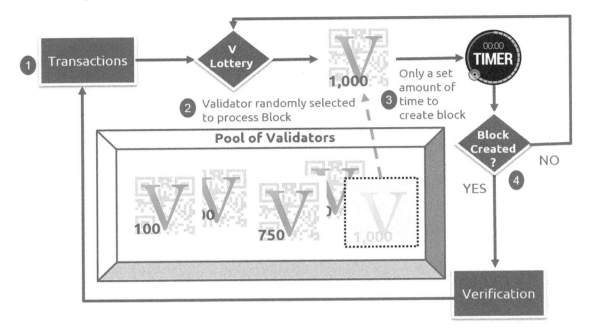

Figure 47 - Proof of Stake process flow

1. First, transactions become available to be processed by the system.

2. Next, a validator must be selected who will validate the transactions. This is accomplished through a random lottery. Notice that the potential pool of validators shows a number next the large, red "V". This number is the weight that each validator has based on their investment in the local coins. The V with 1,000 next to it has a ten-times better chance of being selected in the validator lottery than the V with the 100 next to it. Think of all the V's in the validator pool as having one ticket to the lottery for every local coin they invested to become a validator. In Figure 47 above, the validator who invested 1,000 coins is the lottery winner for processing this block.

3. Once a validator has been selected based on the random, weighted lottery, the validator only has a certain amount of time in which to validate the block of transactions. The amount of time allotted is set by the system. Each validator has their own "time" at which they are able to mine a block. For example, one validator might be able to mine a block at t + 1 minute, while another can't mine it until t + 2 minutes. If the 1st validator is offline or otherwise fails to mine the block, then the 2nd validator can mine a block at t + 2 minutes, and so on. Effectively, all possible validators are assigned a delay, and they must wait for at least that delay before attempting to mine a block.

4. The timer is checked to see if the validator completed the process in the time allotted. Was the block created? If the answer is *no*, then another validator begins to process. The new validator works to verify the block in the time frame allotted. If they complete the verification, the block gets added to the end of the Blockchain. Then the process starts all over again for the next group of transactions.

Issues with Proof of Stake

Some of the issues with various Proof of Stake systems are:

1. **Subjectivity** – Proof of Stake is considered to be a *subjective* protocol in that different nodes can come to different conclusions about the current state of the Blockchain, and a large amount of social information (i.e. reputation) is required in order to participate. Contrast that with Proof of Work which is *objective* because a new node coming onto the network with no knowledge except the protocol definition and the set of all blocks and other "important" messages that have been published can independently come to the exact same conclusion as the rest of the network on the current state of the Blockchain. As we learned the current state is always the state (or branch) that has the most work invested in it. The deeper discussion regarding weak subjectivity is beyond the scope of this book. An excellent article on this subject, written by one of the Ethereum founders, Vitalik Buterin, can be found at https://blog.ethereum.org/2014/11/25/proof-stake-learned-love-weak-subjectivity//.

2. **Economic Concentration** - financial institutions and other areas of token aggregation, like exchanges, exert control over accepting or rejecting protocol updates. These groups with concentrated holdings use their "stake" to exert their will over the blockchain.

3. **Nothing-At-Stake** – with Proof of Stake algorithms, voting by validators is free, so when presented with multiple side branches or forks, there is no penalty to just vote for all the side options that are in process. We will see in Chapter 8, that the *Casper* version of Proof of Stake attempts to solve this issue using a punitive system.

There are many other consensus algorithms and proof verifications. We will examine several of these in Chapter 6.

CHAPTER 6
Other Proofs

Chapter 6 will examine other proof mechanisms. The proofs in this chapter are not as widely used as Proof of Work and Proof of Stake, but they highlight different approaches to gaining consensus and give several different ideas on how this function can be accomplished. Specifically, the following proofs with be covered:

Proof of Elapsed Time

Proof of Activity

Proof of Burn

Proof of Capacity

Proof of Elapsed Time (POET)

The first alternate proof we will scrutinize is Proof of Elapsed Time. Figure 48 gives the definition of Proof of Elapsed Time.

A Nakamoto-style Consensus that uses a Trusted Execution Environment (TEE) to ensures the safety and randomness of the leader election process. Replaces "work" with Trusted Computing...

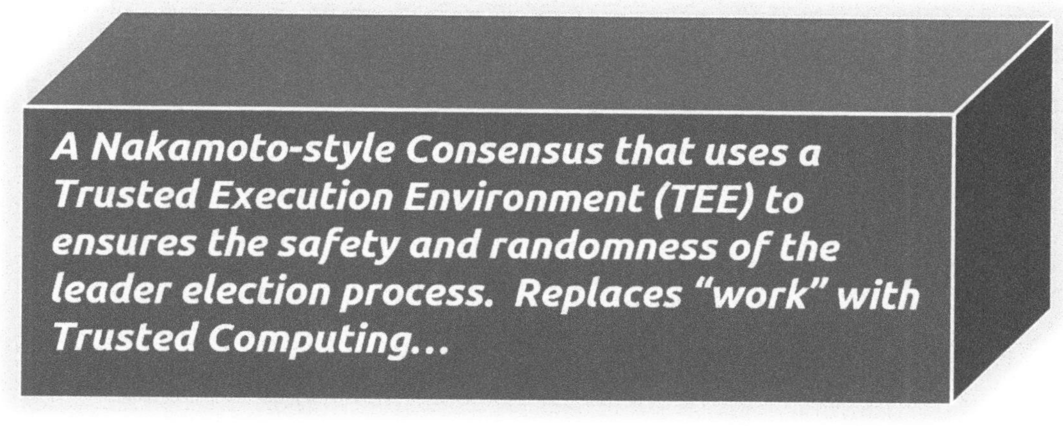

Figure 48 - Proof of Elapsed Time definition

Proof of Elapsed Time is *a Nakamoto-style Consensus that uses a Trusted Execution Environment (TEE) to ensures the safety and randomness of the leader election process. Effectively, it replaces "work" with trusted computing.* The qualities of Proof of Elapsed Time are:

1. This proof method is backed by the giant chip manufacturer, Intel, as part of their Sawtooth Blockchain initiative in cooperation with the Hyperledger project consortium.

2. Proof of Elapsed Time must run in a TEE. A trusted execution environment is a secured area of the processor chip itself. The TEE guarantees the confidentiality and integrity of the code and data that is loaded inside of it. The one offered by Intel is the Software Guard Extensions, or SGX chip.

3. Poof of Elapsed Time uses validators, not miners, similar to Proof of Stake.

4. The proof that Proof of Elapsed Time uses is that the validator waited a specified period of time as opposed to solving a math puzzle as in Proof of Work. One potential consequence of Proof of Elapsed Time versus Proof of Work is a shift in how the investment is made by the miner/validator.

Let's take a look at the process flow of how Proof of Elapsed Time processes transactions.

Proof of Elapsed Time Process Flow

The procedure begins with transactions becoming available to process. A lottery must be made to randomly choose the validator. In Figure 49, each validator is shown with the large red "V". Notice that next to the V is the Intel logo since each validator must be running in a Trusted Execution Environment of the Intel SGX processors.

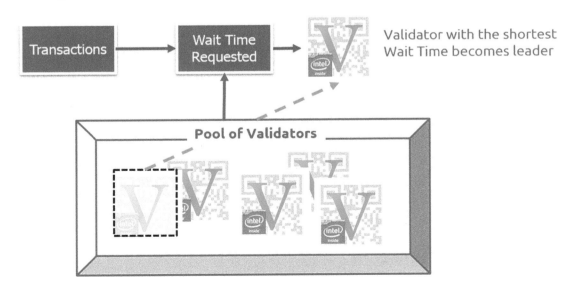

Figure 49 - Proof of Elapsed Time lottery mechanism

Each of the validators requests a random wait time from the system. The wait-time request is a "trusted function" in the TEE. The validator with the shortest wait time for a particular transaction block is elected the leader. In Figure 49 above, this is the validator on the left-most side of the diagram.

Once the validator is selected, see Figure 50 below for the rest of the steps to the Proof of Elapsed Time process flow.

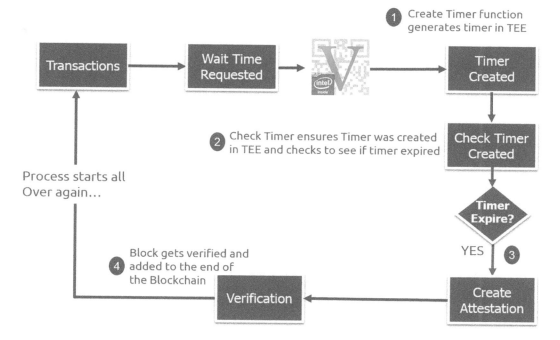

Figure 50 - Proof of Elapsed Time process flow

1. A "create timer" function generates a timer for the transaction block that is guaranteed to have been created inside the Trusted Execution Environment and matches the wait time assigned to the leader.

2. A "check timer" function is then initiated which validates that the timer was, indeed, created in the Trusted Execution Environment and checks to see if the timer has expired.

3. Once the timer expires, the check timer function creates an attestation that confirms that the validator did, in fact, wait the allotted time before claiming the leadership role.

4.   The leader validator then verifies the block and adds it to the end of the blockchain. Then the process starts all over again.

The Proof of Elapsed time meets the criteria for a good lottery algorithm in that it randomly distributes leadership election across the entire population of validators. The probability of election is proportional to the resources contributed (in this case, resources are SGX processors with a Trusted Execution Environment). Further, the low cost of participation increases the likelihood that the population of validators will be large, increasing the robustness of the consensus algorithm. The obvious flaw with Proof of Elapsed Time is that everyone has to trust Intel not to create a rogue SGX environment where they are able to take control of the network by forging timer expirations.

Proof of Activity

The next proof we will review is Proof of Activity. See Figure 51 below for a definition of Proof of Activity.

A hybrid approach that combines both Proof of Work and Proof of Stake to offer an incentive to Bitcoin Miners after all the Bitcoins have been mined...

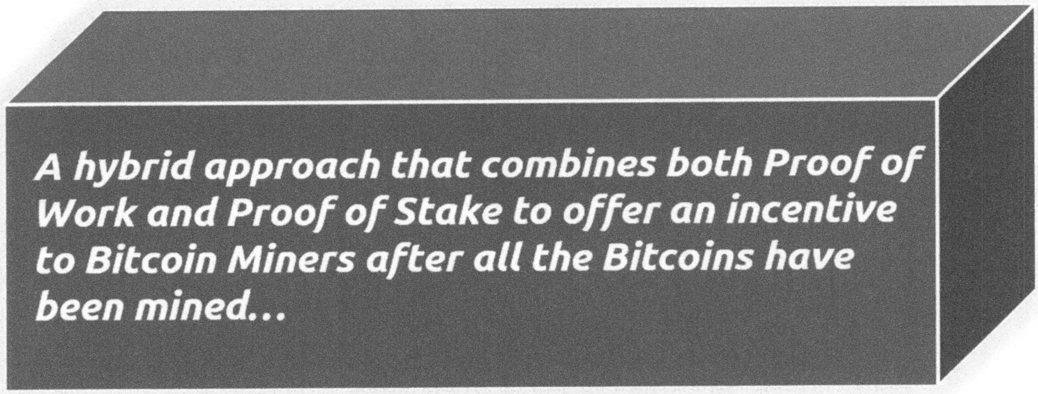

Figure 51 - Proof of Activity definition

Proof of Activity is *a hybrid approach that combines both Proof of Work and Proof of Stake.* Currently, Decentralized Credit (**Decred)** is the only cryptocurrency using a variation of Proof of Activity.

Remember, in Chapter 4, when Proof of Work was reviewed, we discovered that the miners receive two forms of payment for their work whenever they successfully mine a block:

1. Newly minted bitcoins – As of November 2017, miners receive 12.5 newly created bitcoins. When Bitcoin was first created, the reward was set at 50 bitcoins per block mined. The code specified that every 210,000 blocks mined (approximately every four years) that the new coin reward would be cut in half, until it eventually is reduced to zero after 64 halving events.

2. Transaction fees – each transaction that was included in the verified block includes some amount of a transaction fee as a reward for the successful miner. The reward per transaction varies as users can give more incentive to miners to ensure that their transaction is included in a block as quickly as possible. Recall from Chapter 3 when the work flow of how a Bitcoin transaction was reviewed, that the inputs to a transaction must equal the outputs. In our example, the output was 1 bitcoin less than the input. This one "missing" bitcoin would be picked up by the successful miner as a transaction fee.

To avoid hyperinflation, which happens when too much of a currency floods the system, Bitcoin will only ever produce 21 million coins. That means, at some point, the Bitcoin block reward subsidy will disappear, and Bitcoin miners will only receive transaction fees. Some have speculated that the halving of the Block Reward subsidy might cause security issues resulting from a "tragedy of the commons', where people act in their own self-interest and not in the best interest of the system.

Another issue that Proof of Activity attempts to solve is the consolidation of the overall Miner capacity into fewer and fewer Miners. According to the chart in Figure 52 below, published by Buybitcoinworldwide.com in July of 2017, almost 55% of the Bitcoin mining is performed by four companies.

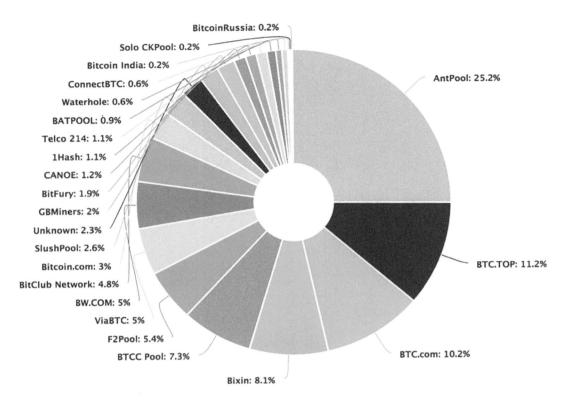

Figure 52 - Worldwide Mining Capacity of Bitcoin – Source: Buybitcoinworldwide.com, July 2017

This is not the one computer – one vote type of consensus that Satoshi Nakamoto envisioned when he penned the Bitcoin white paper. So, Proof of Activity was created as an alternative consensus approach to alleviate the shrinking incentive for Bitcoin miners and allow more nodes to become miners without having to invest in specialized ASIC hardware to help dilute the concentration of the overall mining capacity.

Proof of Activity Process Flow

Refer to Figure 53 below to follow the first part of the Proof of Activity process flow.

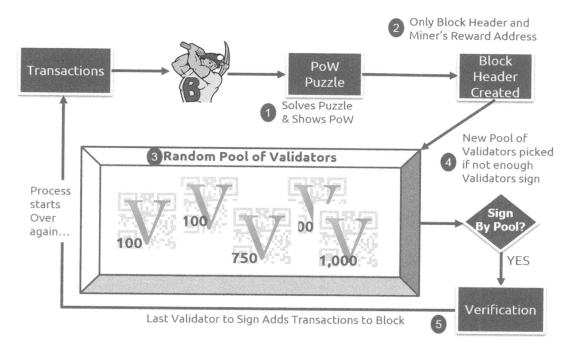

Figure 53 - Proof of Activity process flow

1. Just as with Proof of Work, ten minutes' worth of transactions are presented to the network for processing. The miners work to solve the math puzzle.

2. After the miner solves the math puzzle, the data that gets transmitted to the network is only a template with the block header and the miner's reward address. It is *important* to note that there are *no* transactions in the block (yet!). A number of such templates might appear.

3. A random pool of validators is generated from the block hash by equating the 256 pseudorandom bits of the hash to numbers. Each number corresponds to a single public key of its current owner. This is how N number of random owners are selected as validators.

4. If one or more of the selected validators is unavailable (or does not mine for other considerations) then another new "template" with different sets of signer-candidates is selected for validation, forming an entirely new pool of validators.

5. Once all the validators sign with their public keys, then the block "template" becomes a full-fledged block with the transaction data included. The block-reward is shared between the successful Proof-of-work-miner and the various validators. Then the process starts all over again.

Proof of Activity introduces additional communication overhead and encourages the Proof of Work and Proof of Stake miners to collude for mutual benefit. Proof of Activity is primarily about incentivizing full nodes to be run and providing stakeholders with an incentive to hold tokens. Proof of Activity provides no security improvement over Proof of Work.

Proof of Burn

Now let's examine Proof of Burn. Figure 54 below gives the definition for Proof of Burn.

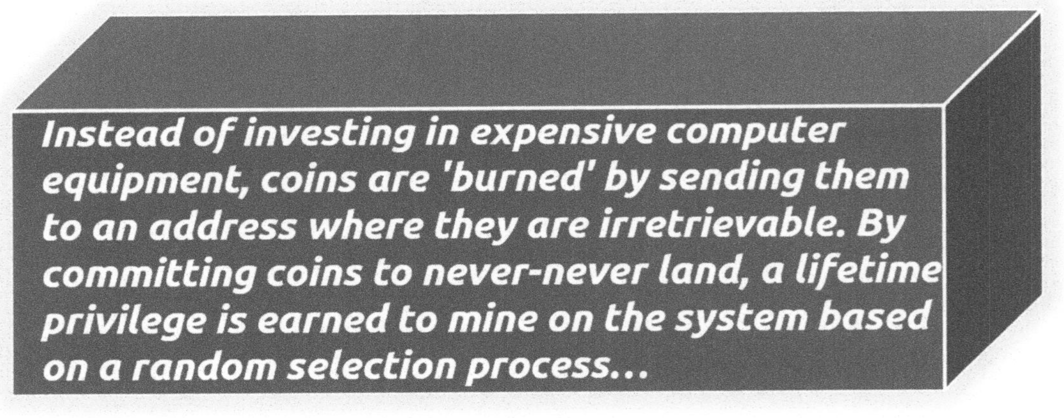

Figure 54 - Proof of Burn definition

With Proof of Burn, instead of investing in expensive computer equipment, coins are "burned" by sending them to an address where they are irretrievable. By committing coins to an invalid key so the coins are, effectively, "burned" - a lifetime privilege is earned to mine on the system based on a random selection process.

Before looking at the process flow for Proof of Burn, there are several ideas surrounding the proof that must first be understood:

1. The first consideration is that in order to become a miner on a Proof of Burn Blockchain, you must first burn some coins. Coins get "burnt" by creating a transaction that sends them to a special burn address that doesn't have a signature key, making the coins irretrievable. Depending on how Proof of Burn is implemented, miners may burn the native currency of the blockchain or the currency of an alternative chain, like Bitcoin.

2. The hash of the burnt transaction is recorded separately to identify the miner in subsequent actions.

3. As part of the random selection process of the miner in Proof of Burn, a burnt hash multiplier is calculated by looking at the number of blocks that have been added to the Blockchain since the creation of the miner's burn transaction. The multiplier is inversely proportional to the total amount of coins burned. This multiplier increases the chances of the miner being selected to process a block. And, as more blocks are added since the miner burned their coins, the multiplier will get smaller and smaller, effectively causing the burnt coins to "decay" which reduces the odds that the miner will be selected. So, eventually, a miner will want to burn more coins to, again, increase their odds of being selected in the lottery. This mimics Bitcoin's mining process, where you have to continually invest in more ASIC computing equipment to maintain hashing power.

4. Finally, the burn hash target is generated for the entire network and is based on the number of burnt coins at the time. The burn hash target is stored in the block in the form of "burn bits" (might I say, embers?). This burn hash is fixed and equal for all the nodes on the network.

Let's take a look at the Proof of Burn process flow.

Proof of Burn Process Flow

Refer to Figure 55 below to follow the Proof of Burn process flow.

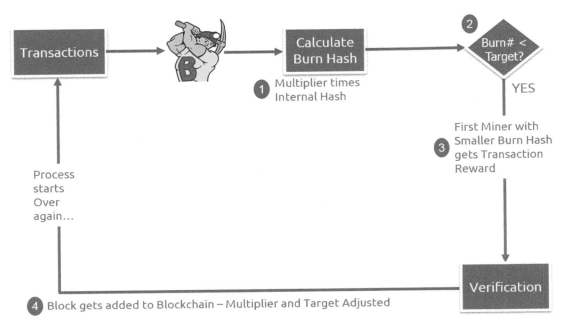

Figure 55 - Proof of Burn process flow

1. Transactions are broadcast to the network. The miner then calculates the burn hash by taking their internal hash from their burn transaction times the multiplier.

2. Then the resulting Burn hash is compared to the system target. If the burn hash is not less than the target, then another miner will be considered.

3. The first miner with a burn hash that is less than the target hash gets the transaction reward, processes the Block, and sends on for verification.

4. After the block is verified, it gets added to the end of the Blockchain and the multiplier and system target are adjusted. The process then starts all over again.

While Proof of Burn is an interesting alternative to Proof of Work, the protocol still wastes resources needlessly by having to solve the iterative math puzzle. Another criticism of Proof of Burn is that "mining power" simply goes to those who are willing to burn more coins.

Proof of Capacity

Remember that with every consensus algorithm, the miner/validator has to invest something in order to be able to process blocks. With Proof of Capacity, the investment is in hard-drive space. Figure 56 below gives a definition of Proof of Capacity.

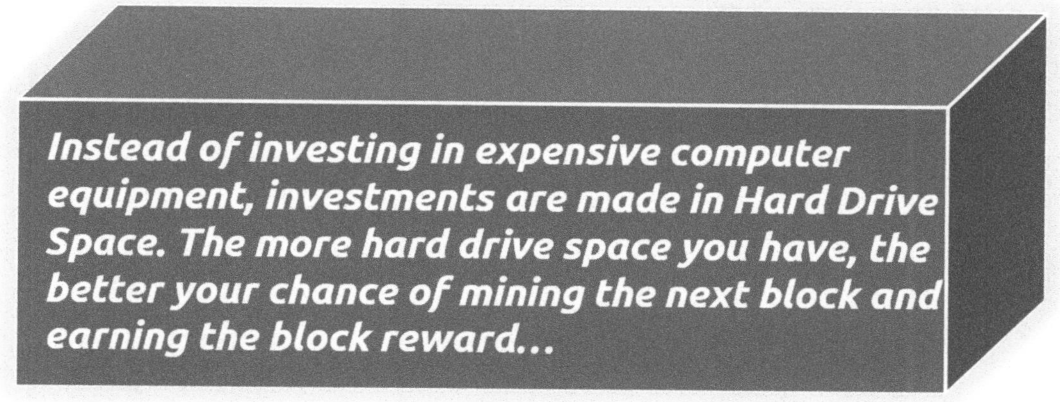

Instead of investing in expensive computer equipment, investments are made in Hard Drive Space. The more hard drive space you have, the better your chance of mining the next block and earning the block reward...

Figure 56 - Proof of Capacity definition

Instead of investing in expensive computer equipment or burning coins, investments are made in disc drive space. The more disc drive space you have, the better your chance of mining the next block and earning the block reward. Burst Coin is the only cryptocurrency using Proof of Capacity at the moment.

Before mining can begin, disc drive space must be committed by the miner. Each Miner must download a *Plotter* algorithm which will subdivide the plot into some number of 256 KB chunks of data known as "scoops". See Figure 57 below for the depiction of the output of the Plotter algorithm.

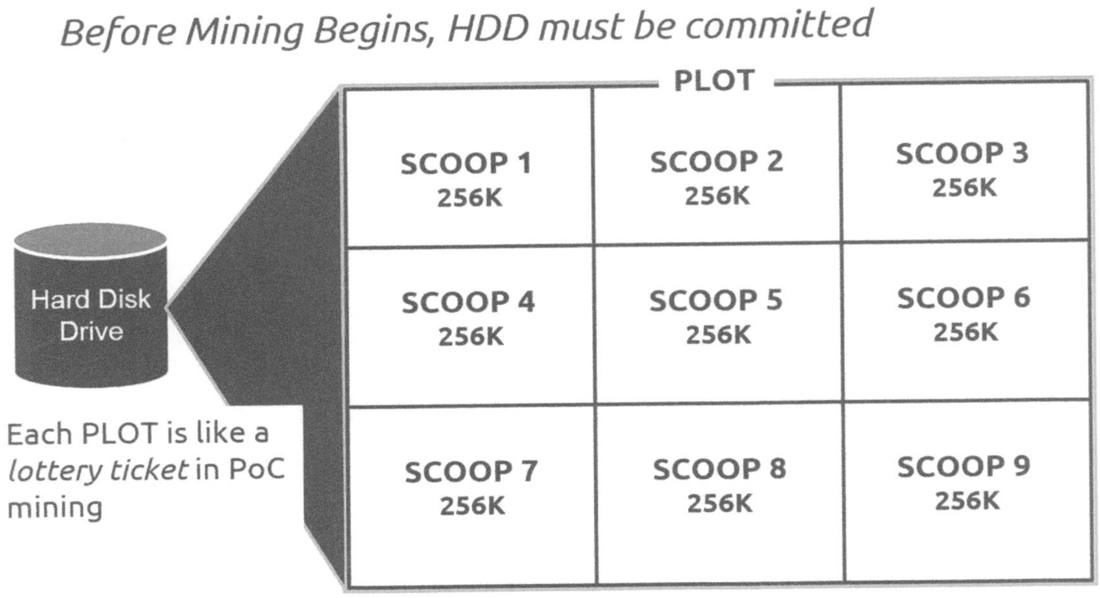

Before Mining Begins, HDD must be committed

Each PLOT is like a *lottery ticket* in PoC mining

Figure 57 - Plotter Algorithm Output

The number of scoops that will be created is a function of the amount of disc drive space the miner is committing to the process. The data in each plot is calculated by repeatedly hashing the miner's public key and a valid nonce. However, not all of the nonces attempted to be hashed will be considered valid and a new nonce will then be tried. This continual checking of new nonces is the *Proof of Work* that proves that many calculations went into finding the correct nonces. With Proof of Capacity, miners do this work once, up-front, during the plotting process and save the results which they can continue to use for each block without needing to continuously redo the work. This is a key difference between Proof of Capacity and Proof of Work.

The more disc drive space allocated, the more scoops the miner has or, said a different way, each plot is like an additional lottery ticket to increase the miner's chances of being selected to mine a block. Now let's look at the Proof of Capacity process flow.

Proof of Capacity Process Flow

Figure 58 below shows the process flow for Proof of Capacity.

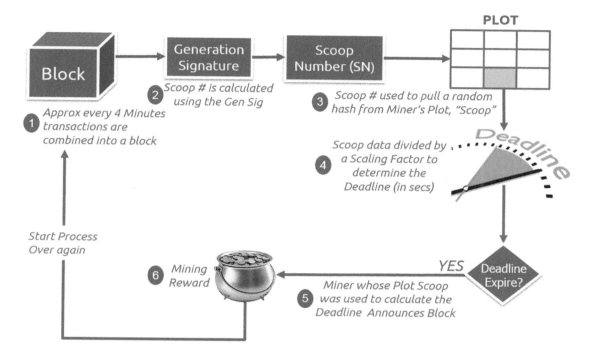

Figure 58 - Proof of Capacity process flow

1. Approximately every four minutes, a group of transactions are combined into a block.

2. While mining, the miners use the signature of the successful miner of the previous block (known as the previous generation signature) to cryptographically combine with the Blockchain height. This produces a random number that is reproducible by the rest of the network and is known as a "scoop number".

3. The scoop number is in turn used to pull a scoop from the miner's plot field.

4. Each miner calculates a deadline based on one of the 4096 scoops of each of their plots as per the calculated global scoop number and the current difficulty. The resulting number is a deadline measured in seconds. This deadline is like a countdown to when that particular miner is able to assemble, sign, and submit a new block to the network.

5. As soon as that many seconds have passed since the last block without a new one having been announced, the miner whose address/nonce combination was used to generate that plot/scoop is eligible to announce a new block and earn the transaction fees associated with the block.

6. The successful miner and earn the transaction fees associated with the block. Then the sequence starts all over again.

Proofs Summary

The chart in Figure 59 below summarizes the five elements of consensus that were identified when we began our discussion on consensus in Chapter 5.

Type of Proof	Investment	Selection Process	Proof Element	Threat Profile
Proof of Work	ASIC's	1st to Solve Puzzle	Hash < System Target	51% Attack
Ripple	-	UNL of Proposer Server	80% of UNL Consensus	Sybil
PBFT	-	Group Consensus	67% Network Consensus	Sybil
Capacity	Disk Storage	Random Scoop Selection	Lowest Deadline	Nothing at Stake
Burn	Crypto-coins	Burn Hash < System Target	Burn Hash < System Target	Nothing at Stake
Elapsed Time	TEE	Shortest Wait Time	Expired Timer < System Target	Intel, Nothing at Stake
Stake	Local Coins	Weighted Random Selection	40% Consensus	Sybil, Nothing at Stake
Activity	ASIC's	PoW is a random oracle to select the PoS miner	Hash < System Target	51% Attack

Figure 59 - Proofs summary

The first of those five elements is the *type of proof*. Figure 59 shows the list of eight proofs that were covered so far in this book. This is not an exhaustive list and new proofs are being tried every day, and in Chapter 9, two more proofs will be examined.

The second element is *investment*. This refers to the investment that miners or validators must make in order to participate in the consensus process. In some cases, the investment is in powerful hardware ASICs and in other cases, the investment is in disc storage, or crypto coins, or specialized SGX processors.

The third element is *selection process* – this refers to the random process that the various proofs use to ultimately select the miner or validator who will process the block and add it to the end of the blockchain. The creativity here is great but all of these options have one thing in common: the selection process has to be truly random.

The fourth element is the *proof element* itself. What must the miners or validators do or what level of agreement must be reached to create a block?

The final element is the *threat profile*. What about the particular proof insulates the network from various nefarious attacks? The details of each of these threat profiles is beyond the scope of this book but plenty of background reading in this area can be found on the web.

Proof of Proof, Segregated Witness, and Side Chains

In Chapter 7, we will examine three different concepts that add capabilities, and in the case of segregated witness, capacity to the Blockchain environment. Specifically, the concepts of Proof of Proof, segregated witness and side chains will be studied.

Proof of Proof

Proof of Proof is not in itself a proof element. Proof of Proof enables blockchains to inherit Proof-of-work security from other Blockchains, creating an ecosystem wherein security originates on established Blockchains, like Bitcoin, and extends to other Blockchains. Some of the advantages of Proof of Proof are:

1. Adds the mathematical proof of Proof of Work to the "trusted" proofs like Proof of Stake. This gives an additional layer of hardened proof to any other consensus algorithm.

2. Allows for selected Proof of Proof intervals to match the critical nature of the application. In other words, not every transaction or block in a Blockchain needs to have the additional Proof of Proof capability but, depending on the critical nature of the Blockchain data, the Proof of Proof miner can process blocks as frequently as needed.

3. Proof of Proof increases auditability because additional validations against the parts of the blockchain that correlate to the Proof of Proof data can be made.

4. Gives new (or smaller) public and private Blockchains the breadth and robustness of the Bitcoin network to prove their work. Through the Proof of Proof approach, all the nodes of the Bitcoin environment become unknowing participants in the Proof of Proof Blockchain. This can be significant since a brand new Blockchain environment may only be a handful of network nodes, but is able to inherit the strength of the Bitcoin Proof of Work algorithm.

Consensus Blockchains

With Proof of Proof, more than one Blockchain is involved. Figure 60 below illustrates the various Blockchains involved with Proof of Proof.

Figure 60 - Proof of Proof Blockchain participants

The first Blockchain participant in the Proof of Proof environment is the Consensus Providing Blockchain (CPB). This is the blockchain that will *add additional security* to the alternate blockchain's process. Currently, this Consensus Providing Blockchain is the Bitcoin blockchain.

The next Blockchain participant is the Blockchain that will *inherit the benefit of the extra security* through Proof of Proof. These are called the Consensus Inheriting Blockchains (CIB). In this example, we show several of the popular blockchains but *any* Blockchain could be a Consensus Inheriting Blockchain.

The last blockchain in this process is the Proof of Proof blockchain that provides the connection between the other two Blockchains.

Proof of Proof Processing

The fundamental goal of Proof of Proof is to *enable a consensus inheriting Blockchain to inherit the complete Proof of Work security of a consensus providing Blockchain.* However, the Proof of Proof process should *not*:

1. Impose any non-trivial limitations on the consensus-inheriting Blockchain. In other words, the blockchains taking advantage of Proof of Proof should not have to change anything about the way blocks are processed in their environment.

2. Require the permission of the consensus-providing Blockchain or the involvement of its Blockchain Miners. So, conversely, just as the consensus-inheriting Blockchain should not be impacted by Proof of Proof, neither should the consensus-providing Blockchain.

3. Leave the consensus-inheriting Blockchain non-functional in the event that the consensus-providing Blockchain fails.

Also, non-mining users of the consensus-inheriting network should not have to interface with the consensus-providing Blockchain network and should not be required to hold any native tokens of the consensus-providing blockchain network.

Proof of Proof Processing Flow

Refer to Figure 61 below for the Proof of Proof process flow.

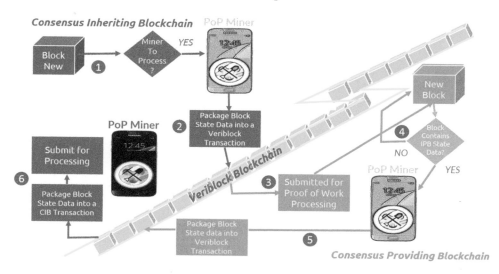

Figure 61 - Proof of Proof processing flow

1. A new block gets created in the consensus-inheriting Blockchain environment. The Proof of Proof miner can decide to process this block or not depending on system settings and miner availability.

2. If this block is not processed, a new block will get created. If the Proof of Proof miner decides to process that block, then the state data from the current block along with the miner's identification is packaged by the Proof of Proof miner, placed into a VeriBlock transaction and the VeriBlock Blockchain gets updated. By capturing the state data in the VeriBlock Blockchain, there is no limit as to the size of the data that can be captured. Notice that this new kind of miner, the Proof of Proof miner, is designated with a cell phone image to show how lightweight the requirements are and that anyone can be a Proof of Proof miner!

3. The inheriting Blockchain's state data is then packaged into a Bitcoin transaction and submitted for processing along with other transactions. Just as a reminder, see Figure 62 below which recaps the Proof of Work process flow that was discussed in Module 5. So, as part of this process, all the mining calculations and verification's that were discussed will eventually be performed on a block that includes the state data from the consensus-inheriting Blockchain.

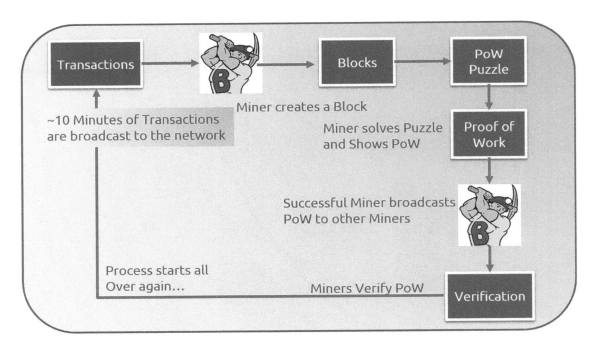

Figure 62 - Proof of Work processing flow refresher

Now the Proof of Proof miner waits to see which block on the Bitcoin network will include the state data from the consensus-inheriting Blockchain. If the latest block in the consensus-providing Blockchain does not contain the consensus-inheriting state data, then the next block will be checked.

When a block is produced in the consensus-providing Blockchain that contains the state data, certain elements of the Bitcoin block are captured by the Proof of Proof miner and are brought back to the VeriBlock blockchain.

The State data from both the VeriBlock Blockchain and the consensus-providing blockchain are packaged and submitted for processing in the consensus-inheriting blockchain.

When the state data captured by the Proof of Proof miner becomes part of a block in the consensus-inheriting Blockchain, it will cause any bad actors who want to illegally fork the blockchain to have to fork *all three* Blockchains: the Bitcoin blockchain, the VeriBlock blockchain *and* the consensus-inheriting Blockchain in unison.

In Figure 63 below, a Proof-of-proof scenario is depicted where there are three blockchains involved: the consensus-inheriting blockchain which is noted as the alt-chain in this example, the VeriBlock blockchain, and the consensus-providing Blockchain which is shown in this example as Bitcoin.

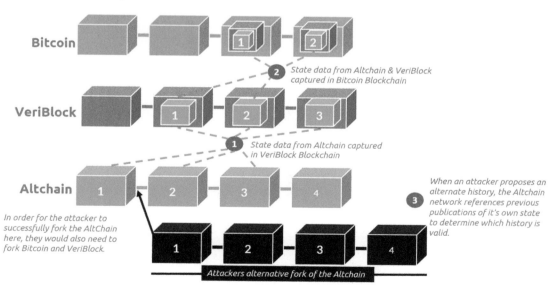

Figure 63 - Proof of Proof Attack Prevention

1. As was described earlier, certain state data from the alt-chain, consensus-inheriting Blockchain gets captured in the VeriBlock Blockchain.

2. Then, both the state data from the consensus-inheriting blockchain along with state data from the VeriBlock Blockchain get updated into the Bitcoin, consensus-providing Blockchain.

3. When an attacker proposes an alternate history, the alt-chain references previous publications of its own state data to determine which history is valid.

In order for the attacker to successfully fork the alt-chain, they would also need to fork both Bitcoin and VeriBlock's Blockchains as well. This would be impossible. This extra fortification against attacks is why an alt-chain would want to use Proof of Proof.

Segregated Witness

We are going to shift gears away from consensus and focus on a couple of topics that you will have, most certainly, heard about. The first is the idea of Segregated Witness. *"Segregated Witness" is a recent update to the structure of Bitcoin transaction data that separates the signature portion of transactions from the data portion, eliminating the transaction malleability problem of Bitcoin and increasing the size of the Bitcoin blocks.* Let's take a look and see exactly what changed in the Bitcoin data structure with the introduction of Segregated Witness.

Reference Figure 64 for an image of the data structure of Bitcoin transaction data before Segregated Witness.

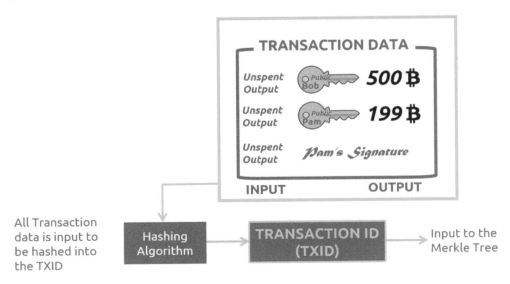

Figure 64 - Bitcoin transaction data structure before Segregated Witness

You will recall from Chapter 3 that the transaction data is made up of inputs and outputs as shown here. Notice in the output field, the validation or public keys are included along with the signature of the person or persons whose coins are being transferred. When validating the transaction, the public key is checked to ensure it has the correct hash (matching the account) and then the signature is checked to ensure it is valid for the transaction and made with the supplied public key. From that point on, the public key corresponding to the address is publicly known. This transaction data is then input to the hashing algorithm to generate a transaction ID. The transaction ID is further input to create the Merkle tree.

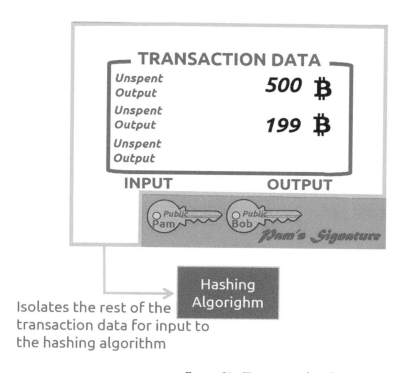

Figure 65 - Transaction data format with segregated witness

With the introduction of Segregated Witness, all of the signature data is moved to the *end* of the transaction data block as depicted in the red square in Figure 65 above.

With the signatures isolated at the end of the data block, the system is now able to input *just* the transaction data into the SHA256 hashing algorithm for calculating the transaction ID. But, *what about the signature data?* If signatures have no effect on the makeup of the transaction ID, then the blockchain no longer serves as proof that the correct signatures were included in transactions.

To ensure that signatures were still traceable to the proper transactions in the Blockchain, Segregated Witness added an extra step to the process. In Figure 66 below, you can see that the creators of Segregated Witness borrowed a technique that was already used in processing blocks by creating a Merkle tree out of the Segregated Witness [signature] data. How Merkle trees are built was covered earlier in this book at the very end of Chapter 2.

To build a signature Merkle tree, the signatures for the transactions are hashed to deliver a signature ID. These signature ID's in turn are hashed in pairs and then those hashes are hashed again until, ultimately, there is only one hash – the signature Merkle root.

So, the picture in Figure 65 above needs to be changed slightly as show in Figure 66 below to show the addition of the *Signature Merkle Root* from the Signature Merkle Tree is input along with the transaction data to be input to the SHA256 hashing algorithm to determine the Transaction ID.

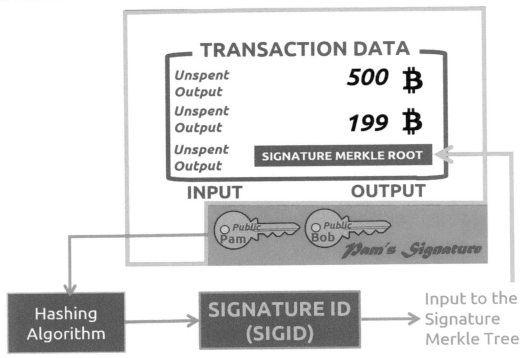

Figure 66 - Signature Merkle root added to transaction data

Then the Block building process finishes as usual with the Transaction ID being used to build the Merkle tree *for the block*. By adding the signature Merkle root to the transaction data output, the signatures are bound to the transaction and also impact the makeup of the Blockchain.

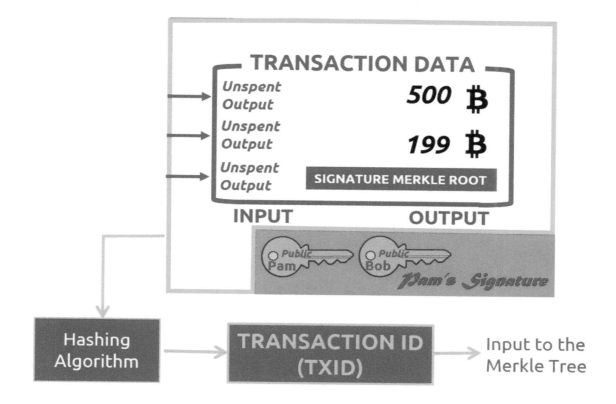

Figure 67 - Signature Merkle root included along with transaction data to form the transaction ID

Benefits of Segregated Witness

There are two primary benefits of Segregated Witness: One was eliminating transaction malleability and the other was increasing the block size of the Bitcoin block. Transaction malleability is a limited denial of service attack and refers to the fact that a transaction's ID can be changed by altering a signature hash in the transaction. Thus, while uncommon, it is possible for a node on the network to change a transaction that was sent in such a way that the transaction ID hash is invalidated.

See Figure 68 below for an idea of how transaction malleability can affect the transaction ID. Here we show that before Segregated Witness, the signatures were input along with the transaction data to create the transaction ID. Remember, due to the distributed nature of Blockchain, there are many nodes that will also process this Block. Notice in the second transaction box, that a node has altered the signature hash for Pam which is designated by

Pam's key changing color. Any node on the network, if they choose to, can change the TXID by making a small change to the signature hash before passing it on. Remember, when hashing was discussed in Module 2, that *any* change to a text string – even one bit – will cause the resultant hash to be completely different. The change to Pam's signature causes the transaction ID to be different from the first (real) transaction ID.

Fixes Transaction Malleability

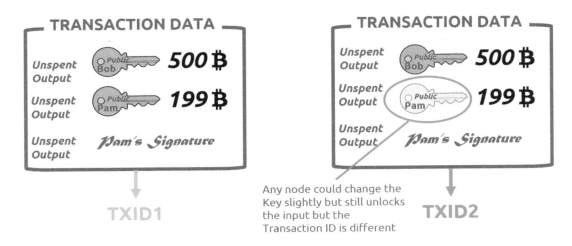

Figure 68 - Transaction malleability issue

Keep in mind that this just changes the transaction ID hash - the output of the transaction remains the same and the bitcoins will go to their intended recipient. Transaction IDs are particularly important because, as a global ledger, Bitcoin is organized around these transaction IDs. As we reviewed in Chapter 3, when a Bitcoin transaction flow was explained, new transactions refer back to past transaction IDs to prove that the person sending bitcoins, indeed, has the balance available to do so. Having the wrong transaction ID will affect that process.

As we saw earlier with Segregated Witness, the signature data is not used in calculating the transaction ID, so it is no longer possible to alter it, thus eliminating the possibility of the transaction malleability problem as shown in Figure 69 below.

Fixes Transaction Malleability

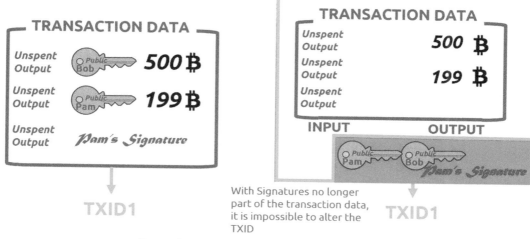

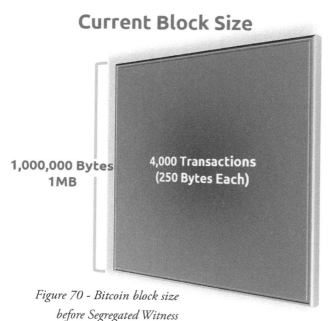

With Signatures no longer part of the transaction data, it is impossible to alter the TXID

Figure 69 - Removing transaction malleability problem with Segregated Witness

Increasing the Bitcoin Block Size

The second benefit of Segregated Witness is an effective increase in the block size limit of the Bitcoin block. Before Segregated Witness, the Bitcoin block was a fixed 1,000,000 bytes or 1 megabyte. As shown in Figure 70 on the left, this means that, for example, if you had transactions that were each 250 bytes in size, you could store 4,000 of those transactions on a block.

Current Block Size

1,000,000 Bytes
1MB

4,000 Transactions
(250 Bytes Each)

Figure 70 - Bitcoin block size before Segregated Witness

With Segregated Witness, the size of a Bitcoin block is based on something called "weight units". Now, there are 4,000,000 weight units that can be stored in a Bitcoin block. The way a weight unit is calculated is for every byte of transaction data, there are four weight units assigned. However, for every byte of signature data, there is only one weight unit assigned which, basically, yields a 75%

discount on how much space signatures occupy in a block - freeing up more space in a block for transaction data.

So, let's take the same size transaction as was mentioned earlier of 250 bytes. Let's assume that the 250 bytes was made up of 200 bytes of transaction data and 50 bytes of signature data. Figure 71 shows the calculation that would be made to determine how many transactions would fit in the Block.

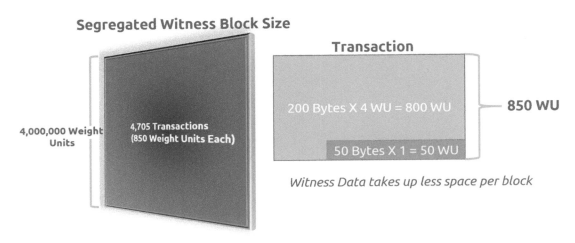

Figure 71 - Increased Block Capacity after Segregated Witness

The number of weight units occupied by that transaction would be 850 which is the 200 bytes of transaction data multiplied by four and the 50 bytes of signature data multiplied by one. The net effect is that witness data takes up less space per block. With a transaction size of 850 Weight Units, you could store 4,705 transactions on a block. So, in this example, with identically-sized transactions, an extra 705 transactions were able to be stored on a block after implementing Segregated Witness.

Sidechains

The idea of sidechains has existed and has been floating around the blockchain environment for quite some time now. The basic idea with sidechains is to extend the decentralization of trust into other Blockchains, and to other digital assets. Basically, a sidechain is *any mechanism that allows tokens from one Blockchain (main chain) to be securely used within a completely separate Blockchain (sidechain) but [the tokens] can still be moved back to the original chain if necessary.* Sidechains are also referred to as alternate Blockchains, or alt-chains – sometimes referred to as alt-coins. Let's take a look at the motivation for why sidechains are needed.

Why are Sidechains Needed?

The idea of a sidechain began due to limitations in the original Blockchain, Bitcoin. Bitcoin's objective is relatively simple: use its Blockchain to support the transfer of a single native digital asset, which is not redeemable for anything but bitcoin. Keeping the objective modest and straightforward allowed for many simplifications in the implementation of Bitcoin, but resulted in various tradeoffs. Bitcoin was limited in the following ways:

1. Bitcoin was not scalable.
2. Emphasis on security at any cost.
3. Limited scripting language.
4. Trade something other than bitcoin.
5. Slow process for making functional changes to the Bitcoin platform.
6. No data privacy.

Scalability - The first of these limitations is scalability. Currently, Bitcoin can process six transactions per second which is too slow for many applications. Part of this scalability issue is due to the time that it takes for miners to solve the math problem (10 minutes). Reducing the complexity of the math problem that miners have to solve would allow the network to support higher transaction rates, improving scalability, but at a cost of placing more work on miners. Coping with the extra workload could lead to a centralization risk where more and more mining power is concentrated in fewer and fewer miners.

Security - A second tradeoff is security versus cost. Bitcoin stores every transaction in its history with the same level of immutability. This becomes expensive to maintain and is not appropriate for low value or low-risk transactions. Ideally, each transaction should have the flexibility to determine how its historical records are handled, as transactions vary widely in value and risk profile. But, Bitcoin, by design, supports only a "one size fits all" solution which leads people to look for alternatives like sidechains.

Scripting Language - Also, Bitcoin's functionality is limited in many ways. One of the glaring limitations is in Bitcoin's scripting language - which could be expanded to be Turing-complete which would allow for the possibility of creating smart contracts.

Trading other Assets - There are assets besides currencies and Bitcoin that many people, and organizations want to trade on a blockchain, such as land deeds and other tokenized assets.

Implementing Changes to the Platform – With the inevitability of change in any new technology, Bitcoin inspired many new ideas as the concept gained acceptance. However, there is consensus amongst Bitcoin developers that changes to Bitcoin must be implemented slowly, cautiously, and only with clear acceptance from the entire Bitcoin community. Even if there is a pressing need to add new features, there is no safe upgrade path for Bitcoin, in the sense that all participants must act in concert for any change to be affected. So, many turned to sidechains to implement features not imagined when Bitcoin was first developed.

No Data Privacy - Sometime, the parties to a transaction do not want all their transaction details stored in a public ledger for all to see. Many want an option for private transactions which Bitcoin does not provide.

After reviewing the list above, it is clear to see that the motivation to introduce sidechains was to overcome some of these shortcomings. Sidechains share the Bitcoin codebase, except for modifications to the code to address the one or more of the concerns discussed above.

Sidechain Process Flow

To see how sidechains interact, let's follow the process flow between a parent chain and a sidechain as depicted in Figure 72 below.

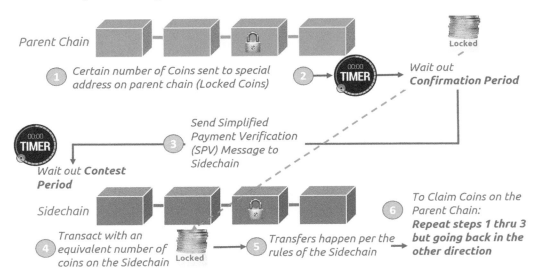

Figure 72 - Sidechain process flow

1. A certain number of coins in the parent chain are sent to a specially formed Bitcoin address. The address is specially designed so that the coins will now be out of the owner of the bitcoin's control - and out of the control of anyone else either. The coins are considered "locked" (shown by the lock icon in the Figure) until such time that somebody can prove they have rightful ownership of the coins.

2. The locked coins must now wait for a "confirmation period" to expire. This is a duration for which a coin must be locked on the parent chain before it can be transferred to the sidechain. The purpose of the confirmation period is to allow for sufficient work to be created on the Bitcoin blockchain. A typical confirmation period would be on the order of a day or two.

3. The user then sends a transaction to the sidechain. This transaction contains a proof that the coins were sent to that special Bitcoin address, that the coins are therefore now locked, and identifies the rightful owner of the coins. A Simplified Payment Verification or SPV is sent which is composed of a list of block headers demonstrating Proof-of-work, and a cryptographic proof that an output was created. On the sidechain, a contest period, similar to the confirmation period on the parent chain must expire before the coins can be used. A contest 9eriod is a duration in which newly-transferred coins may not be spent on the sidechain. The purpose of a contest period is to prevent the possibility for double-spending.

4. Once the contest period has expired, an equivalent number of coins is made available on the sidechain. And remember: the coins are locked on the Bitcoin network, so no new coins have been created or destroyed - the coins have effectively been "moved".

5. An important point to understand is that the coins are transferred on the sidechain *following the rules of the sidechain and taking advantage of any extended features of the sidechain.* The coins could be transferred to one or several new owners.

6. The logic to transfer the coins from the sidechain back to the parent chain is symmetric. So, at any point, whomever is holding these coins on the sidechain can send them *back* to the parent chain network by performing steps 1 through 3 – sending coins to a special address that puts a "lock" on the coins on the sidechain; waiting out the confirmation period on the sidechain and contest period on the parent chain; and providing a sufficient Simplified Payment Verification to unlock the coins back at the parent chain.

7. The last step is not shown in Figure 72 above. After the contest period on the parent chain, the coins will disappear from the sidechain and become available again on the Bitcoin network. However, the coins are now under the control of whoever last owned them on the sidechain, not the original owner.

While there are many sidechains or altcoins in existence, they have their own set of issues. First, there is the notion of "infrastructure fragmentation". Infrastructure fragmentation is the idea that because each sidechain uses its own technology approach, effort is frequently duplicated and lost. The companies developing sidechains may lack certain domain knowledge like security, so security problems are often duplicated across sidechains while the corresponding fixes are not. This lack of standardization leads to chaos. Imagine trying to drive rental car where every car had the gas and brake pedals in a different location. This would not be a viable situation, and neither is the current environment of sidechains.

A second problem is that sidechains typically have their own native cryptocurrency, or altcoin, with a floating price. To access the sidechain, users must find a way in the market to obtain the related currency, exposing them to the high risk and volatility associated with new cryptocurrencies. Finally, the requirement to independently solve the problems of initial coin distribution and valuation, while at the same time contending with the challenges of standing up a Blockchain in a crowded, competitive market, encourages companies to be preoccupied with their cryptocurrency valuation instead of focusing on technical innovation.

Ideas like Proof of Proof, Segregated Witness, and sidechains are all attempts to bring more innovation to the Blockchain world – and this is only the beginning.

CHAPTER 8
Smart Contracts and Oracles

In Chapter 8, we will study smart contracts and learn what is an oracle and when oracles are needed as it relates to the smart contract environment.

Smart Contracts

The idea for a smart contract has been around since 1994 when Nick Szabo, a legal scholar and cryptographer, realized that the decentralized ledger could be used for smart contracts, otherwise called self-executing contracts, digital contracts, or Blockchain contracts. Refer to Figure 73 for a definition of Smart Contracts.

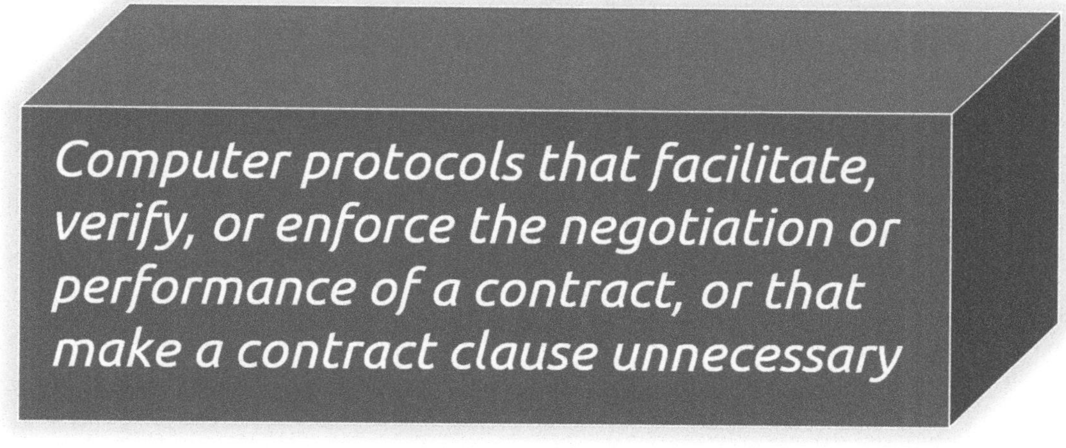

Computer protocols that facilitate, verify, or enforce the negotiation or performance of a contract, or that make a contract clause unnecessary

Figure 73 - Smart contract definition

In this format, contracts are converted to computer code called scripts, stored and replicated on the system and supervised by the network of computers that run the Blockchain. This concept of smart contracts is increasingly important in the information age as it increases an enterprise's compliance ability by ensuring that contracted commitments comply with required terms and conditions.

Paper vs. Coded Contracts

The main differences between the traditional paper contracts with their typical "legalese" and smart contracts which are encoded in a Blockchain. Figure 74 below shows a summary of the differences:

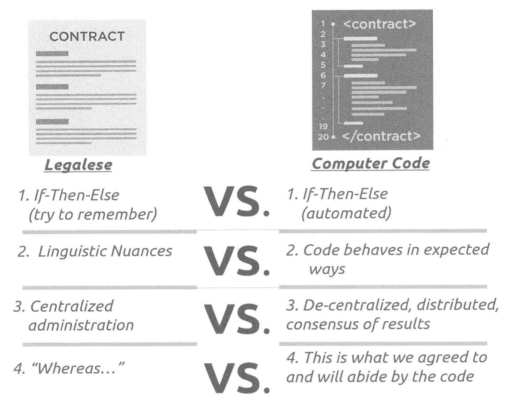

Figure 74 - Paper versus coded contract differences

1. First, with paper contracts, all the conditions of the contract are on a piece of paper and after the ink dries, the specifics of the contract begin to fade from memory. If there are specific demands mandated by the contract , you have to try and remember to do those things to remain in compliance of the contract. With an encoded contract, the compliance is automated as the code will be executed consistently whenever the conditions stated in the contract are met.

2. The next contrast is the linguistic nuances of the paper contract which can be left open for, potentially, different interpretations. Contrast this with the consistent execution of smart contract *code* which behaves the exact same way in every instance.

3. Paper contracts are locked up in a desk or contract management system and are only referenced when something comes into question. Smart contracts, on the other hand, are distributed across the entire Blockchain network and as transactions are made involving the smart contract, the code is executed and the results subject to the consensus of the network nodes in real time.

4. Finally, to bridge the paper contract with the encoded contract, the normal paper contract can have all the "whereas" clauses that lawyers enjoy. Then a clause in the paper contract points to a smart contract on a Blockchain saying, "This is what we both agree to run and we will abide by the results of the code." If, somehow, the results turn out to be unacceptable, both parties will have to live with the consequences as they signed off on the code results in the contract.

Smart Contract Benefits

Anything requiring a signature could become a smart contract. Smart contracts deliver specific value when compared to their paper counterpart as listed below:

1. *Increased Trust* – Because all the documents are encrypted on a shared ledger, the level of trust regarding the contract obligations increases. There is no way that someone can say that they lost the document!

2. *Increased Backup* - Along the same vein, smart contracts provide an increased level of backup. First, there are multiple copies of the contract document itself replicated across the many nodes of the Blockchain. It's impossible not to have a copy of the original. On the Blockchain, each and every node has your back. Equally as important is the fact that the *code* itself is locked and replicated across the nodes of the Blockchain. This means that no one can tamper with the code once it is accepted on the Blockchain.

3. *Increased Savings* - Smart contracts lead to savings since they eliminate the need for an intermediary. You would, for instance, have to pay a notary to witness your transaction in a traditional setting. Smart contracts will also save the time it takes to acquire and then verify physical signatures. Consider an international shipment where signatures are collected as merchandise is moved from the manufacturer, to the trucking company, to the loading docks to the shipping company, etc. The same information can be captured through smart contracts as data is collected along the way, eliminating the need for physical signatures.

4. *Increased Autonomy* - Smart contracts lead to increased autonomy. Businesses know the type of agreement they want to make; there's no need to rely on a broker, a lawyer or other intermediaries to confirm the agreement. Incidentally, this also eliminates the danger of manipulation by a third party, since execution is managed automatically by the network, rather than by one or more, possibly biased or dishonest, individuals.

5. *Increased Accuracy* - Smart contracts are not only automated, faster and cheaper, but they also avoid the human errors that come from manually filling out heaps of forms.

Oracles

Oracles are trusted entities that provide smart contracts with information on the state of the world *outside* of the Blockchain. So, whatever outside information might be the focus of some smart contract terms - like commodity price, exchange rates, package temperature, flight departure information, or any other external information - an oracle is the means that will connect smart contracts to "provably honest" data sources. Smart contracts are touted as having the potential to do all kinds amazing things. But, to fulfill their promise, there needs to be a way for a smart contract to communicate with and access data from the outside world. This is where oracles come into play. Due to the nature of a Blockchain, smart contracts can't just fetch data that exists outside the blockchain on their own. But, oracles come with their own set of challenges.

Challenges for Oracles

To start with, an oracle needs a reliable data source. They need to be able to provide an accurate and tamper-proof source of information. So, if a smart contract offers insurance against flight cancellations, it is important to make sure that the data you are receiving on flights is accurate, and has not been altered at any point after being accessed from the website. Also, following the distributed network Blockchain principles, the data that is retrieved by oracles would, ideally, be accepted and agreed upon by the network participants. This shows that there is consensus from the Blockchain network on the accuracy of the data.

Confidential queries present another challenge for oracles. Assume a smart contract needs information on a private broker account statement or a medical record. A query from the oracle to the account or medical website would need to contain login, password or other personal and private information. Most people are uncomfortable having this information replicated around a Blockchain network. We will see various approaches to dealing with these challenges when the three different types of oracles are studied here.

Types of Oracle Implementations

There are three general types of oracles: software-based, consensus-based, and hardware-based. The general characteristics of each is described in Figure 75 below:

There are 3 Types of Oracles:

Oracle Type	Type of Source Data	Attestation of Data Origin
Software-Based	Near-Real-Time Internet	TLSNotary / Pagesigner
Consensus-Based	Predictive	Group Consensus
Hardware-Based	Real-Time, User-Centric	Crypto Attestation on Sensor

Figure 75 - Three types of oracles

Software-based oracles access data in near-real time over the Internet. When the knowledge of the information you are seeking is available online, simple software-based oracles can provide efficient solutions. Software-based oracles can answer questions such as: "What is the value of Bitcoin in Euro?", "Did this plane suffer a delay of more than 30 minutes?" or "Was it raining yesterday in Detroit?". When reliable data is available online, on the Internet, and can be extracted from trusted sources such as company, airlines, financial data aggregators or weather institutes, then software-based oracles are the mechanism to retrieve that information. However, there needs to be *proof* that the data retrieved from the Internet really came from the source identified and has not been tampered with since the data was accessed. This type of attestation is achieved through a service called TLSNotary and specific function called, PageSigner. We will see exactly how this works in the next few pages.

Consensus-based oracles try to take advantage of the "wisdom of the crowd" type of information. Decentralized prediction markets such as Augur.com heavily rely on oracles to settle outcomes of events. However, to avoid market manipulation, these oracles cannot be based on the trust of one single entity. The solution is to use rather complex consensus mechanisms based on reputation, ultimately building decentralized oracles.

Hardware-based oracles are the last type of oracle. The data collected here is real-time, user-based information. So, information collected from temperature sensors, or other sensors can be gathered in real-time by using specialized hardware-based oracle devices. The data retrieved from this type of device is verified using a crypto-attestation on the sensor itself. Let's look at how each of these oracles work.

Software-based Oracles Data Flow

Refer to Figure 76 below to see the process flow of a smart contract that needs to employ a software-based oracle.

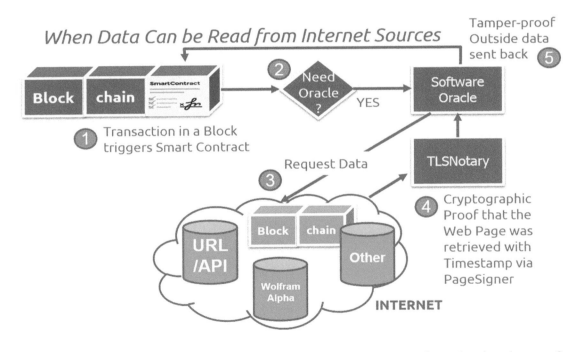

Figure 76 - Software-based oracle process flow

98

When a transaction in the Blockchain references a smart contract (we will see exactly how this works in a few pages), the smart contract must determine where the data that is involved with checking the conditions of the contract is located.

Is it available inside the blockchain? Or, does the data reside somewhere on the Internet? If the data needs to be retrieved from the Internet, then a software-based oracle is needed.

The data would then be requested from the Internet source, whether it was a specific company web site or a data search site, like Wolfram Alpha, or even another Blockchain.

The retrieved data is passed through the TLSNotary function called "PageSigner". PageSigner allows you to "notarize" web pages. Think of it as a cryptographically secure webpage screenshot - it's different from an ordinary screenshot in that it can't be edited in Photoshop; it really *proves* that you received that data from the server. It also puts a timestamp on the page so that information can be used, if necessary, in fulfilling smart contract terms and conditions.

The data retrieved from the Internet, along with the associated PageSigner attestation, is passed back to the smart contract script to verify the compliance to terms and conditions of the smart contract.

Consensus-based Oracle Data Flow

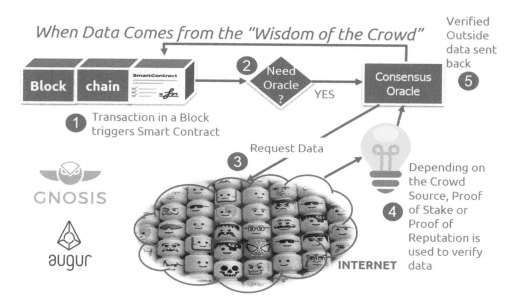

Figure 77 - Consensus-based oracle process flow

The flow for a Consensus Based oracle starts out exactly the same as the flow for the software-based oracle. Refer to Figure 77 above for a view of the consensus-based Oracle process flow.

1. When a transaction in the blockchain references a smart contract, the smart contract must determine where the data that is involved with checking the conditions of the contract is located.

2. Is it available inside the Blockchain? Or, does the data reside somewhere on the Internet? Furthermore, does the required data need come from a prediction site on the Internet? If the data needs to be retrieved from there, then a consensus-based oracle is needed.

3. The data would then be requested from one of the predictive or forecasting Internet sources like Augur and Gnosis.

4. Depending on the source of the data, the result will be attested through a standard consensus method like Proof of Stake. The Gnosis predictive site uses crowd-sourced wisdom to make predictions and uses Proof of Stake to attest to the result. If Augur, which is a distributed forecasting site that also uses the wisdom of the crowd, is referenced for the data, then the Proof of Reputation consensus method will be used to attest to the result.

5. The data retrieved from the corresponding site is passed back to the smart contract script to verify its terms and conditions.

Hardware-based Oracle Data Flow

Again, the flow for a hardware-based oracle starts out exactly the same as the flow for the software-based and consensus-based Oracle. Refer to Figure 78 below for a view of the hardware-based oracle process flow.

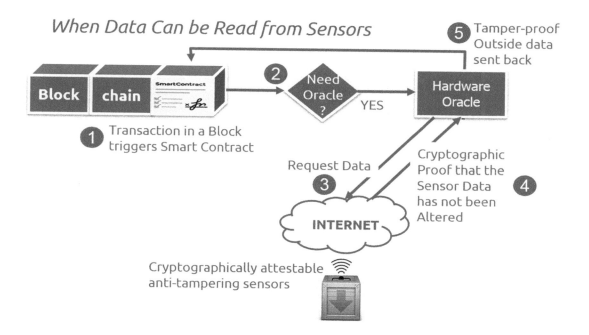

Figure 78 - Hardware Based Oracle Process Flow

1. When a transaction in the Blockchain references a smart contract, the smart contract must determine where the data that is involved with checking the conditions of the contract is located.

2. Is it available inside the Blockchain? Or, is the data being collected by a hardware sensor? If the data needs to be retrieved from a specialized hardware sensor, then a hardware-based oracle is needed.

3. The data that had been collected by the hardware sensor and stored on the Internet would then be requested.

4. As the data is private, accuracy of the information cannot be confirmed by either a public feed nor by consensus. A specialized sensor device is needed that includes cryptographic verification of the data. See Figure 79 below for a look inside of a specialized sensor device.

5. The cryptographic proof that the data has not been tampered with, and the data from the sensor is passed back to the smart contract script to verify its terms and conditions.

A Look Inside the Sensor Device

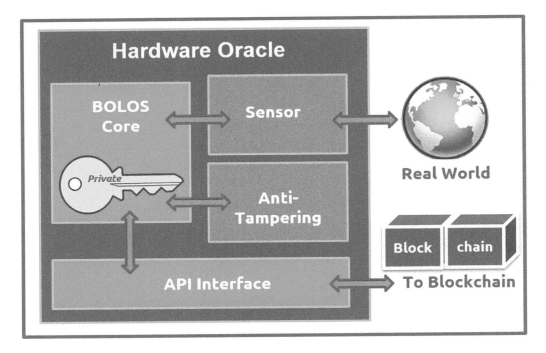

Figure 79 - A look inside a BOLOS core sensor

A look inside the sensor device reveals that in addition to the **sensor** itself that is collecting real-time information from the outside world, there are several other components loaded in the device. To be able to securely report a reading from any kind of sensor, the combination of the following is necessary:

1. First, a cryptographic attestation of the sensor reading authenticating the origin of the information being measured by the sensor is needed. This type of attestation can be delivered from any device with a *Blockchain Open Ledger Operating System* or (BOLOS) core. This **BOLOS core** provides building blocks for cryptographic security with tools and an **API Interface** for building Blockchain-aware applications on the device itself. Each device has a **private key** for signing and authenticating outgoing data payloads. Also, a nonce is added to the payload message to avoid sending duplicate information.

2. Next, an **anti-tampering** installation of the reader device must be present. The anti-tampering device will render the sensor inoperable by erasing the private key in case of a manipulation attempt from an outside attacker. For example,

if the sensor became connected to another object, or something tried to inject false stimuli like an attack on the device, then the private key would be erased, disabling the device from further processing.

Smart Contract Process Flow -No Oracle Needed

You will recall that earlier in this chapter we made the point that the terms of smart contracts have been converted to computer code called scripts. See Figure 80 below to follow the process flow for how a smart contract is triggered and then the follow-on logic to enforce the smart contract conditions.

Example 1: No Oracle Needed

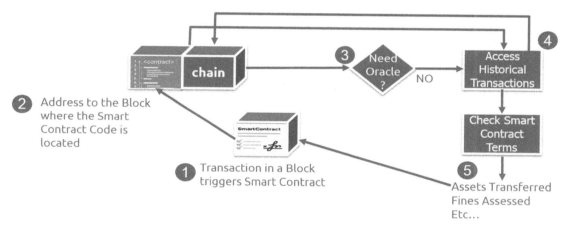

Figure 80 - Smart contract process flow - no oracles needed

1. The smart contract scripts are compiled into low-level executable code and stored at a specific address in a particular block in the blockchain. Any transaction that references that specific address is a signal to the blockchain that that smart contract should be invoked as part of the processing for this transaction.

2. Remember that there are many nodes in a Blockchain network, so the distributed virtual machine on every full node executes the script's operation code using the data which is sent with the transaction.

3. As the smart contract executes, the determination must be made whether or not an oracle is needed.

4. If the data needed to confirm the smart contract terms is contained in the Blockchain itself, then historic data is retrieved.

5. Using the historical blockchain data, the actual terms and conditions of the smart contract are checked. If the conditions are met (or not met) the appropriate action is taken, whether that is the transfer of an asset, the assessment of a fine, the charging of fee, or *whatever* the smart contract was written to do.

Smart Contract Process Flow with Oracles

Figure 81 shows the process flow that a smart contract would take when an oracle is needed to access information from the world outside of the Blockchain.

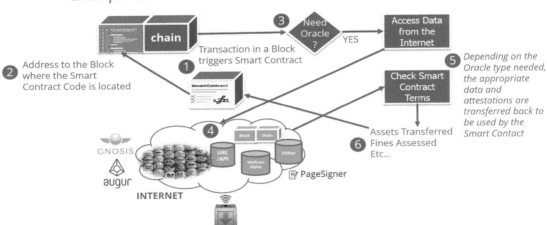

Figure 81 - Smart contract process flow with oracles

1. As we saw in the previous Smart Contract process flow diagram, any transaction that references the address to where the Smart Contract code is located is a signal to the Blockchain that that Smart Contract should be invoked as part of the processing for this transaction.

2. The many nodes in the Blockchain network executes the script's operation code using the data which is sent with the transaction.

3. As the Smart Contract executes, the determination has to be made whether or not an Oracle is needed.

4. As the Smart Contract is being processed, it is determined that some information is needed from outside the Blockchain through the Internet. Depending on the kind of data needed by the Smart Contract, the appropriate Oracle is invoked to securely retrieve the data.

5. If the information needed is from a general Web site or another Blockchain, then a Software Oracle would be invoked and the attestation of the data authenticity and timestamp are provided by the TLS Notary function, PageSigner. If the data needed is from a predictive web site like Gnosis or Augur, then the consensus methods used by those two sites would be used to confirm the Wisdom of the Crowd information that is provided. Finally, if the information required by the Smart Contract is real-time, non-public, user-centric information, like the kind of information gathered through specialized sensors, then a Hardware Oracle would be used.

6. Next the actual terms and conditions are checked using the information gathered from the Oracle-sourced data. If the conditions are met (or not met) the appropriate action is taken, whether that is the transfer of an asset, the assessment of a fine, the charging of fee, or whatever the Smart Contract was written to do.

Smart Contract Application Example

Consider a commercial deal which involves a dozen different companies and many diverse data-driven interactions throughout its life. In a traditional environment, the IT departments for the commercial entities would likely structure the administration of the data driven aspects of the deal by establishing a tracking system completely under the control of that particular commercial entity. In a best-case scenario, some programmatic interface would be provided for the other participating companies in this scenario to query records or send new information regarding a current transaction. It is highly likely that each of these dozen commercial entities would each also establish a similar system to monitor and track the data interactions over the lifetime of the deal.

Compare the approach above with the much more streamlined process needed if the dozen different companies had decided to use a Blockchain. The execution certainty of smart contracts, married with the historical transaction certainty of a Blockchain, would be extremely interesting for business partners involved in this transaction scenario. If the commercial entities were wise about how they structured the deal, they could track every data-driven interaction with a smart contract-enabled Blockchain. This would save the work of having to build twelve different systems; ensure the interoperability and interfaces between the systems; and the duplicate labor needed to appropriately categorize and file relevant transactional data. Every entity having access to the distributed Blockchain would be able to completely verify the entirety of all the interactions between the parties as well as the entire history of the data, which would be automatically maintained over the life of the deal and summarized at its conclusion.

This concludes Chapter 8 regarding smart contracts and oracles. Chapter 9 will cover the leading Blockchain approaches currently in the market.

CHAPTER 9
Leading Blockchain Approaches

In Chapter 9, several leading Blockchains and Blockchain companies on the market will be reviewed. By now, you should now have the background on Blockchain to be able to clearly see the rationale for the various approaches to using Blockchain used by the different companies discussed in this chapter.

Blockchain Pedigree

Based on the white paper written by Satoshi Nakamoto in 2009, the idea of Bitcoin was born. At the time, not much attention was paid to the underlying infrastructure that supported Bitcoin, called blockchain. As Bitcoin came to market, it proved the viability and robustness of Blockchains. But there were other capabilities that were demonstrated that were never before accomplished in the computing world like anonymous, trustless transactions between parties who might not even know or trust each other and consensus across nodes that were distributed around the world. But, Bitcoin was very one-dimensional in that it only allowed for the trading of bitcoins and nothing else. Figure 82 below shows a Blockchain pedigree diagram or a Blockchain family tree, if you will.

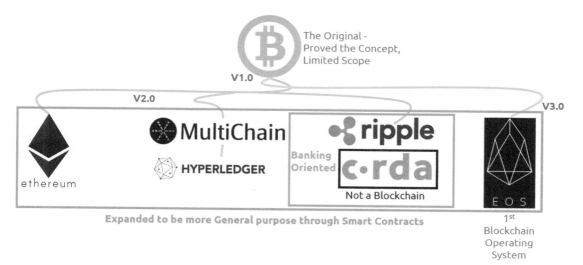

Figure 82 - Blockchain family tree (for now)

At the top of the tree is the original Blockchain, Bitcoin. As the code base for Bitcoin was open source, several innovators took the code and began to add capabilities on top of the original code base.

If you follow the green lines coming out of the Bitcoin logo in Figure 82, you will find "version 2", if you will, of Blockchain. These version 2 Blockchains were filled with many diverse approaches. However, several Blockchains added the capability of smart contracts which were not possible with Bitcoin. The blockchains that are inside the large red box all support some form of smart contract. Smart contracts were the biggest addition that these second and third generation blockchains added over what Bitcoin brought to the market. Smart contracts allowed these blockchains to be more general purpose and not be locked into just financial market applications.

The Blockchain that broke out from the pack of early adopters was Ethereum for several reasons which will be reviewed shortly. On the other hand, MultiChain provides a platform from which an organization can build their own blockchain very quickly or extend the Bitcoin Blockchain. Also, some of the largest corporations like IBM, Linux, and Intel formed the HyperLedger Foundation to build Blockchains that were more industrial strength to appeal to Fortune 1000 companies. Still, other companies like Ripple and Corda, stuck to the original Bitcoin roots and focused purely on the financial markets with their offerings. These two companies are grouped in the green box in Figure 82. The financial markets are huge around the world, and Ripple and Corda chose to place their focus only there.

The next version of Blockchain, version 3.0, is just coming to the marketplace in October of 2017. If you follow the gold line out of the Bitcoin logo in Figure 82, it leads to EOS, which promises to be the first Blockchain "Operating System". EOS's approach is to focus on providing low-level services like role-based security, indexed databases, and advanced messaging to the developers who build their applications on top of EOS. Supplying these low-level services allows developers to focus more on application functionality and not have to write the code for system services.

Finally, you will notice that Corda is shown in Figure 82 in a black box with the notation "not a Blockchain". Of all the Blockchains listed in Figure 82, only Corda has gone so far off in their own direction that, technically, Corda is not actually using Blockchain or distributed ledger technology (DLT). Rather, R3, the company that created Corda, has chosen to develop what is being described as a "shared ledger" platform where consensus on transactions is reached only between the parties involved in the transaction as opposed to a Blockchain where all transaction data on the ledger must be broadcast to all other participants on the ledger, and all participants must agree on all the facts. R3 believes that in the banking and finance world, this network-level consensus raises privacy and scalability issues so a "shared ledger" as opposed to a "distributed ledger" is used.

While there are many Blockchains on the market and new ones being added every day, we will take a closer look at this list of leading Blockchains as we progress through this chapter.

Bitcoin Summary

Following the chronology of Blockchain, let's start with a summary of Bitcoin. Figure 83 below highlights pertinent details regarding Bitcoin.

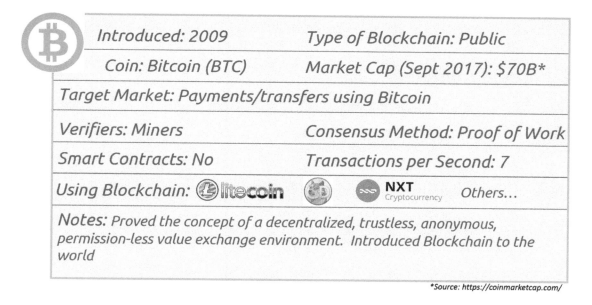

Source: https://coinmarketcap.com/

Figure 83 - Bitcoin summary

As was mentioned earlier, Bitcoin was launched in 2009 by an unknown programmer or group of programmers under the alias of Satoshi Nakamoto. Bitcoin is a public Blockchain meaning that anyone, anywhere in the world can participate in the Bitcoin network. Bitcoin has its own cryptocurrency which trades under the symbol, "BTC". As of September of 2017, Bitcoin has a market capitalization of almost $70 billion USD. The target market for Bitcoin is payments and transfers using only bitcoin.

As was described in Chapter 4, Bitcoin uses miners and Proof of Work as its consensus method. Although Bitcoin has a simple scripting language called Script, it is Turing-*incomplete* meaning that not all logical functions can be coded using Script. Therefore, more complex scenarios like smart contracts are not a part of Bitcoin. Due to the intense Proof of Work processing in Bitcoin, only six transactions per second are possible using Bitcoin. As we discussed in Chapter 8, segregated witness is being added to Bitcoin which should increase the number of transactions that Bitcoin can process per second.

Some other Blockchains that use the Bitcoin base are Litecoin, which is a cryptocurrency that enables instant payments to anyone in the world and that can be efficiently mined with consumer-grade hardware; DogeCoin, which was originally introduced as a "joke" currency but has had over 100 billion coins mined; NXT is a cryptocurrency that uses Proof of Stake instead of Proof of Work, and there are many other blockchains as well. Bitcoin proved the concept of decentralized, trustless, anonymous, permission-less value exchange and introduced blockchain to the world!

Ethereum Summary

Ethereum is easily the most used Blockchain platform on the market. Refer to Figure 84 below which highlights pertinent details regarding Ethereum.

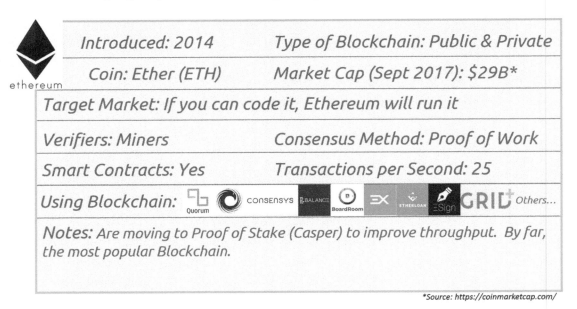

Source: https://coinmarketcap.com/

Figure 84 - Ethereum summary

Ethereum was founded in 2014 by Vitalik Buterin, Dr. Gavin Wood, and Joseph Lubin. The goal of the Ethereum founders was to expand blockchain technology to more than just financial applications. In fact, Ethereum wanted to create an environment where *any* distributed application could be developed. Ethereum supports both public and private blockchain implementations.

Ethereum has their own coin called "Ether" that trades on the cryptocurrency exchanges under the symbol "ETH". The current market capitalization of Ether is $29 billion USD. The target market for Ethereum is very broad, with an attitude "if you can code it, Ethereum will run it". This open-minded approach has led to its broad adoption as we will see in the next few pages.

Ethereum also uses miners and Proof of Work as its consensus method just like Bitcoin. However, as highlighted in the *notes* section of Figure 84, Ethereum is moving away from Proof of Work and moving to a version of Proof of Stake which is code named Casper. The primary motivation for this change is to improve the number of transactions per second that Ethereum can process and reduce the amount of resources consumed by Proof of Work. We will examine Casper in more detail in a few pages.

One of the key elements that Ethereum brought to the table was a Turing-complete scripting language, called Solidity, used for coding smart contracts. Currently, Ethereum can process around 25 transactions per second.

Ethereum is by far the most popular blockchain platform. Several companies are listed in Figure 84 like Quorum, Balance, Boardroom, EX, EtherLoan, E-Sign, and Grid+ that use Ethereum Blockchain. However, the most significant of the companies that use the Ethereum blockchain is Consensys. Consensys was started by one of the Ethereum founders, Joseph Lubin, and the Consensys business model is for Consensys to act as a "hub" that spawns "spoke" ventures through development, resource sharing, acquisitions, investments and the formation of joint ventures. These spoke companies benefit from foundational components built by ConsenSys that enable new services and business models to be built on the Ethereum Blockchain.

Ethereum vs. All Other Alt-chains

To give you an idea of Ethereum's dominance in the marketplace, take a look at the statistics shown in Figure 85 Below:

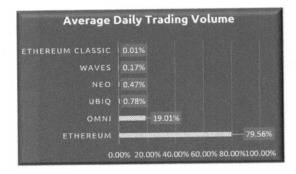

Source: CryptoPortfolio, August, 2017

Figure 85 - Ethereum market domination

Ethereum accounts for almost 80% of the average daily trading volume and 87% of the overall market capitalization of all the non-Bitcoin blockchain companies according to CryptoPorfolio's August 2017 report. And, according to CoinMarketCap, Ethereum dominates the market with 79% of all the assets traded being based on Ethereum's blockchain; 87% of the overall market cap; and 56% of all the companies listed on the exchange have blockchains based on Ethereum. Outside of Bitcoin, no other Bbockchain compares to Ethereum in market adoption.

Ethereum also supports the concept of distributed apps [applications]. Distributed apps are like a smart contract with some distinguishing characteristics:

1. Distributed apps can have an *unbound* number of participants. In a typical smart contract scenario, there are a handful of interested participants for any one contract.

2. Next, these distributed apps don't have to be a financial application. Distributed apps can touch any kind of application setting.

3. And, instead of having to build an entirely separate Blockchain for each distributed app, Ethereum enables the potential development of thousands of different applications, all on the same platform.

Much like Apple has the App Store for iPhone, Ethereum has pushed the development of the distributed apps and keeps an active web page at https://dapps.ethercasts.com/ where you can see all the distributed apps that have been developed to date. Figure 86 below shows a screen capture of some of the available distributed apps as of September 2017.

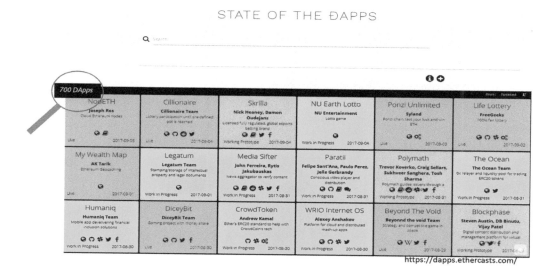

Figure 86 - Distributed Apps Directory

If you zoom in a little, you can see that as of September 2017, there are 700 distributed apps developed.

Casper Proof of Stake

As was noted during the overview discussion on Ethereum, earlier in this chapter, Ethereum is switching its consensus method from Proof of Work to the Casper version of Proof of Stake. Figure 87 below gives a definition of Casper Proof of Stake.

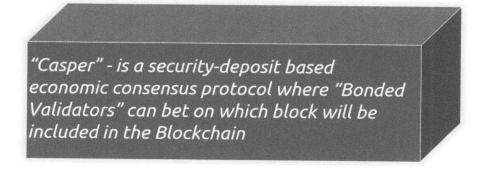

"Casper" - is a security-deposit based economic consensus protocol where "Bonded Validators" can bet on which block will be included in the Blockchain

Figure 87 - Casper Proof of Stake definition

"Casper" - *is a security-deposit based economic consensus protocol where "bonded validators" can bet on which block will be included in the Blockchain.* To implement Casper, Ethereum uses its own smart contract mechanism. Through the Casper smart contract, anyone can enroll to become a block validator, place bets on which version of a block they think will be the ultimate block added to the end of the Blockchain, check the consensus betting activity that is going on at the moment, and withdraw from being a block validator. Nodes become a "bonded" validator by placing a deposit using the Casper smart contract. This is the "stake" that the validators are putting up like we learned earlier in the discussion of Proof of Stake. If a bonded validator behaves badly in doing the block validation job, they can lose their entire deposit.

After nodes are bonded, they can bet on which block will be included on the blockchain going forward. Betting *with* the consensus as to which version of a block is ultimately added to the end of the Blockchain will result in a reward, whereas betting *against* the consensus can result in losses against the bonded validators' deposit. Let's look at a process flow of how Casper works on the next slide.

Casper process flow

Figure 88 below shows the Casper Proof of Stake Process Flow.

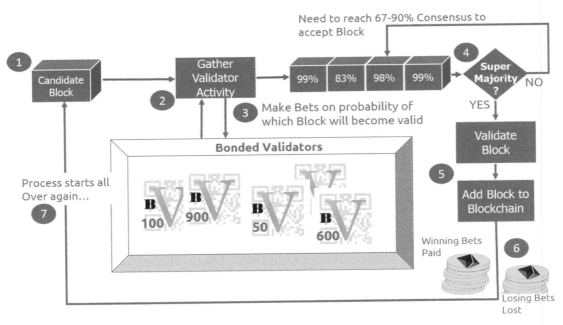

Figure 88 - Casper Proof of Stake process flow

1. A cryptographically-signed candidate block produced by a node is sent out into the network to become finalized.

2. The number next to the red V is the amount of Ether that each validator invested to become a bonded validator. The validators gather as much information as possible from the system about the transactions of other validators. This information is gathered by making calls to the Casper smart contract. Each validator will attempt to stay as up-to-date as possible on the stakes other validators are using to bet on blocks and compile the data.

3. After analyzing the consensus data, bets are made on the probability of which block will become validated. You can see the probability percentage of each bet that is placed.

4. A check is made to see if a super-majority of bonded validators has decided on a block. If the super-majority of between 67 to 90 percent has not been reached, then more betting continues until a super-majority *is* achieved.

5. Once enough bets are made on the same block, that block is sent forward for validation.

6. Once the block is added to the end of the Blockchain, then the bonded validators that bet on the added block are paid on their bet as a mining reward and the bonded validators that bet on a different block will lose their bet for not following the consensus.

7. Then the process starts all over again with a new candidate block.

That is all for this section on Ethereum. Now let's take a look at MultiChain.

Multichain summary

Figure 89 below summarizes the relevant facts regarding MultiChain.

Introduced: 2015	Type of Blockchain: Private
Coin: None	Market Cap (Sept 2017): NA
Target Market: Private Build-your-own Blockchains	
Verifiers: Miners	Consensus Method: Proof of Work
Smart Contracts: No	Transactions per Second: 500+
Using Blockchain: 850+ Downloads	
Notes: Speeds the Proof of Work process by using a "Mining Diversity" algorithm that creates a round-robin approach to who can mine the next block.	

Figure 89 - MultiChain summary

MultiChain was founded in 2015 by Coin Sciences and its founder, Dr. Gideon Greenspan. MultiChain is an off-the-shelf platform for the creation and deployment of private Blockchains either within or between organizations. MultiChain aims to overcome a key obstacle to the deployment of blockchain technology in the institutional financial sector by providing the privacy and control that the financial sector demands.

Multichain supports private Blockchains and does not have its own coin. Therefore, it does not have a definable market capitalization. The target market for Multichain is anyone who wants to build their own Blockchain. Several large consulting companies like Accenture use MultiChain in their blockchain practice.

MultiChain uses a Proof of Work consensus algorithm that has been slightly modified by using a tactic called "mining diversity" which limits how many blocks can be created by the same miner within a given time period. In private Blockchains, where the networks are not so large, mining diversity makes sure that all the consensus is not concentrated in just a few miners.

MultiChain does not support smart contracts but it can reach transaction volumes of 500 transactions per second by allowing users to alter parameters that control how the Blockchain works like block creation time interval - this helps with transaction throughput. Although there have been greater than 850 downloads of the MultiChain code, there are no active Blockchains using MultiChain at this time.

HyperLedger Summary

Figure 90 below summarizes the key facts regarding the Hyperledger Project:

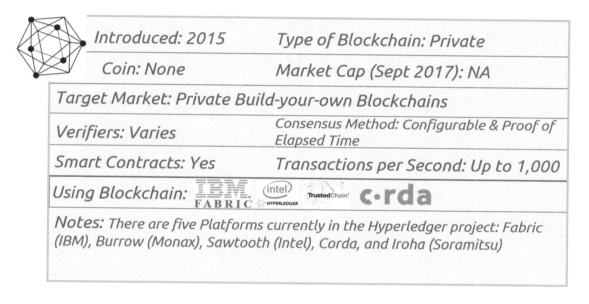

Introduced: 2015	Type of Blockchain: Private
Coin: None	Market Cap (Sept 2017): NA
Target Market: Private Build-your-own Blockchains	
Verifiers: Varies	Consensus Method: Configurable & Proof of Elapsed Time
Smart Contracts: Yes	Transactions per Second: Up to 1,000
Using Blockchain: IBM FABRIC (intel) HYPERLEDGER TrustedChain c•rda	
Notes: There are five Platforms currently in the Hyperledger project: Fabric (IBM), Burrow (Monax), Sawtooth (Intel), Corda, and Iroha (Soramitsu)	

Figure 90 - HyperLedger Project summary

In December 2015, the Linux Foundation announced the creation of the HyperLedger Project. The objective of the project is to develop Blockchains and distributed ledgers, with a particular focus on improving the performance and reliability of these systems as compared to existing cryptocurrency designs. Another goal of the project was to increase the robustness of Blockchain so that they can support the scale and transaction throughput needed by major global companies. HyperLedger supports only private Blockchains.

There is no coin associated with HyperLedger and therefore, no measurable market capitalization. The target market for HyperLedger are global technological, financial, and supply-chain companies who want to have a private Blockchain. Various HyperLedger Project members have contributed Blockchain alternatives to the project, therefore the consensus method varies between a user-defined configurable approach to Proof of Elapsed Time. Smart contracts are supported by the HyperLedger-derived Blockchains. As there are several HyperLedger alternative Blockchains, the transaction throughput varies.

Currently, four Blockchains have been produced through the HyperLedger project. IBM has released a blockchain called *Fabric* around which IBM wraps many of their services like hosting and Blockchain as a service. Intel has released a Blockchain called *Sawtooth* that takes advantage of Intel's SGX Trusted Execution Environment computer chips. Both of these claim transaction throughput speeds up to 1,000 transactions per second. *TrustedChain* is a permissioned Blockchain network of European Trust Service Providers, designed by Ifin Sistemi, the leading Italian company in the sector of trusted services for public administration and banking. TrustedChain was built on the HyperLedger *Burrow* blockchain platform. The last example is *Corda*, whose source code was donated to the HyperLedger Project in October of 2017. R3, the company that created Corda made good on their promise to release their code as open source. So, with the addition of Corda, the HyperLedger Project can offer a shared ledger solution as well as a true Blockchain solution.

In the *notes* section of Figure 90, the five platforms (Blockchains) that are part of the HyperLedger project are listed. The companies that contributed the technology are shown in parenthesis.

Ripple Summary

Figure 91 below shows a summary of the relevant facts about Ripple:

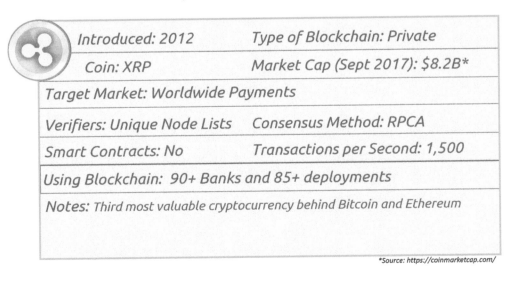

Source: https://coinmarketcap.com/

Figure 91 - Ripple summary

Ripple was conceived in 2004 by Ryan Fugger but did not come to complete fruition until Jed McCalib and Chris Larsen approached Mr. Fugger with their digital currency idea in 2012. Ripple connects banks, payment providers, digital asset exchanges and corporates via RippleNet to provide one frictionless experience to send money globally. Ripple operates as a private Blockchain.

Ripple has its own digital currency called XRP with a symbol also being XRP. The current market capitalization of XRP is $8.2 billion. The target market for Ripple is the worldwide payments and currency transfers. You will recall that the Ripple Protocol Consensus Algorithm (RCPA) was covered in detail in Chapter 6. Using RCPA, consensus comes from achieving 80% consensus within Unique Node Lists.

Ripple does not support smart contracts and the transaction throughput on RippleNet can reach 1,500 transactions per second. As of September 2017, there are 100+ banks using Ripple across 85+ implementations. Ripple is the third most valuable cryptocurrency on the market behind Bitcoin and Ethereum.

EOS Summary

Figure 92 below summarizes the salient points regarding EOS:

EOS	Introduced: 2017	Type of Blockchain: Public/Private
	Coin: EOS (EOS)	Market Cap (Sept 2017): $800M
Target Market: Enterprise Blockchain		
Verifiers: Block Producers		Consensus Method: Delegated POS
Smart Contracts: Yes		Transactions per Second: 10,000
Using Blockchain: bitshares STEEM		
Notes: Being designed as an "Distributed Operating System" for Blockchain with no fees charged to use the system.		

*Source: https://coinmarketcap.com/

Figure 92 - EOS summary

EOS is being developed by a company called Block One, led by experienced Blockchain entrepreneur, Dan Larimer. EOS was introduced in 2017 as the first Blockchain operating system with a focus on being a platform for distributed applications in direct competition with Ethereum. EOS aims to provide all the core functions to application developers and allow them to focus on just the business logic that makes their applications unique. The first version of the product is due to be released by the end of 2017. EOS supports the operation of both public and private blockchains.

EOS has its own digital currency called EOS with a symbol also being EOS. The current market capitalization of EOS is $800 million as of September of 2017 according to Coinmarketcap.com.

The target market for EOS is enterprise-grade Blockchains. EOS uses a modified version of Proof of Stake, called *Delegated* Proof of Stake, where block validation is scheduled or delegated to block producers. We will take a closer look at Delegated Proof of Stake starting in a couple of pages. EOS supports smart contracts and the transaction throughput for EOS can reach 10,000 transactions per second.

As EOS has not been released yet, there are no implementations using it. However, some of the capabilities that EOS will feature, like named accounts and decentralized budget allocation, were proved from two of Dan Larimer's earlier projects, Bitshares and Steem. Bitshares is a decentralized exchange that tracks the value of gold and silver and exchange cryptocurrencies. Bitshares introduce the idea of "named accounts" where a user can use a common name to reference their account and all the cryptographic public and private keys were managed by the system. Steem is the first social media site built on a Blockchain where participants are rewarded for their participation.

In the notes field of Figure 92, it is interesting to understand that, unlike Ethereum—which charges Ether (the Ethereum local coin) to use their platform—users can take advantage of the EOS distributed operating system features without incurring fees.

EOS Blockchain Operating System Features

Some of the unique capabilities that EOS will be bringing to the market are the following:

1. Governance
2. Scalability

3. Free usage

4. Easier upgrades and bug fixes

5. Industrial-strength functions

Let's examine each of these capabilities:

Governance - EOS has its own constitution that everyone must sign off on. This constitution details the peer-to-peer terms of service that exist inside the EOS environment, so everyone knows what to expect and, more importantly, what is expected of them. And, instead of being a formality, this constitution has some teeth as it is legally binding and provides an arbitration mechanism in case of disputes. Also built into the constitution is the option of the EOS community to vote to change the constitution at any time.

Scalability - The EOS system is designed for scalability to support millions of users. This is a big claim, but there is basis to believe this will be the case as one of the other blockchains that Dan Larimer created, Steem, supports millions of concurrent users.

Free usage - EOS allows for free usage of the platform. Users invest in EOS coins and, in return, the users get access to EOS system resources like bandwidth, storage, and CPU cycles in proportion to their holdings. So, if you own 1% of the EOS tokens, you would have access to 1% of the system resources to run your distributed application. So, while EOS tokens are not *consumed* when an application runs in the environment, it does help to have invested in some of the EOS tokens to gain access to system resources to run your application. It should be noted that the "holdings limit" only comes into play when there is contention for resources. If you were the only user on the system, you would have access to all the resources.

Easier Upgrades and Bug Fixes - Upgrades and bug fixes can be applied without forking the system, which has happened with Bitcoin and Ethereum. If an application is broken – like in an infinite loop – or fails, block producers in EOS can freeze the application so there is no need to fork the Blockchain. Also, system upgrades are voted on by the stakeholders and there is no need to hard fork the Blockchain to implement these upgrades.

Industrial-strength Functionality - EOS aims to be industrial strength by taking the distributed apps and the decentralized computers they run on and connecting the two with a robust operating system. Figure 93 below shows the list of industrial-strength functions connecting distributed computers to EOS applications.

The EOS operating system will provide many of the same features and robustness that corporations have come to expect in the pre-Blockchain world, like:

Account management whereby users can identify their accounts through common names and not cryptographic keys.

User-based account permissions where people can have access to application functions based on their role in an organization.

Deterministic parallel processing where functions are evaluated to determine if they can be processed in parallel or must be sequentially processed. For example, transactions need to be processed sequentially while thread allocation can be processed in parallel.

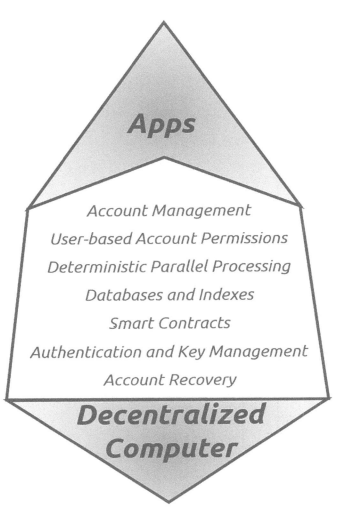

Figure 93 - EOS industrial-strength functionality

Databases and indexes. Each user will have their own database and those databases can be indexed for faster access times.

Smart contract support. EOS will support Smart Contracts.

Authentication and key management will be provided by EOS to ensure identities are properly handled. And, the idea of *account recovery* is built into the system and provides users a way to restore control of their account if their keys are stolen. With offering all of these capabilities, EOS has a real chance to change the course of the Blockchain market going forward.

Delegated Proof of Stake Definition

As was mentioned earlier, EOS uses *Delegated* Proof of Stake as a consensus algorithm. See Figure 94 below for a definition of Delegate Proof of Stake.

Delegated Proof of Stake is where *token holders on an EOS Blockchain select block producers through a continuous approval voting system and the block producers can produce blocks proportional to the total votes they have received relative to all other producers*. Let's examine the characteristics of Delegated Proof of Stake.

Token holders on an EOS blockchain select Block Producers through a continuous approval voting system and the Block Producers can produce blocks proportional to the total votes they have received relative to all other Producers

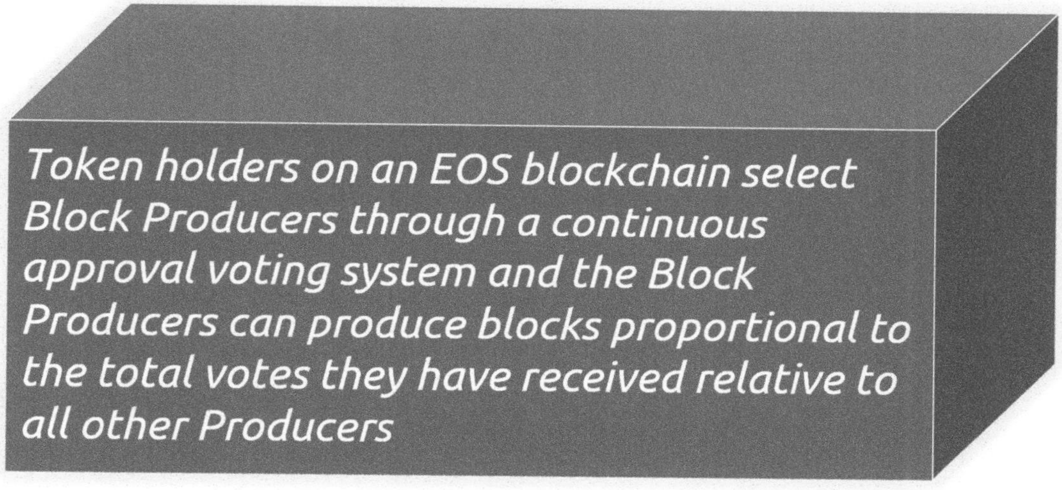

Figure 94 - Delegated Proof of Stake definition

Delegated Proof of Stake Characteristics

With Delegated Proof of Stake, there is exactly one block producer at a time. The benefit of only having one block producer working on a given block at any time is that a Delegated Proof of Stake Blockchain does not experience any branches as we saw with Proof of Work because the block producers *cooperate* to produce blocks rather than compete.

Anyone can become a block producer if they demonstrate that they have the capacity to do so. The top 20 + 1 vote getters become block producers. The top 20 by total approval are automatically chosen for every round of block production and the last block producer (who finished 21st in the voting) is chosen to produce blocks in proportion to the number of votes they received relative to the other block producers. With EOS, validators are separate from block producers to help improve throughput.

Delegated Proof of Stake Workflow

Figure 94 below shows the Delegated Proof of Stake Process Flow.

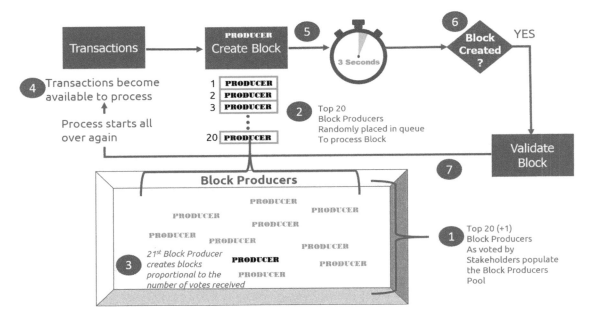

Figure 95 - Delegated Proof of Stake Process Flow

1. Candidate block producers are voted on by stakeholders via a continuous voting process. The top 20 vote getters plus 1 populate the block producer pool.

2. Block producers are placed in a queue in a random order derived from the block time.

3. The 21st Block Producer will participate in block creation in proportion to the number of votes received versus the other block producers. In Figure 93, the 21st vote getter is the lone block producer left in the pool.

4. A batch of transactions become available to be processed.

5. The block producer that is at the top of the queue is the only one to attempt to build this block. All the others are bumped up in the queue so to be ready for the next block.

6. The block producer has three seconds to complete the build of the block. If the block producer did *not* complete the build of the block in the three-second window, then the next block producer in the queue attempts to build the block.

7. If this block producer finishes the block inside of the three-second window, then the block is put forward for validation. Then the process starts all over again.

Evolving Blockchain Summary

Let's summarize our review of the blockchain marketplace. Bitcoin was the first Blockchain in the market and proved the concept. But everyone, including Bitcoin, has looked to make improvements on the original design. These initiatives for improvement revolve around creating better transaction throughput and extending the scripting language to be Turing-complete.

Ethereum has had very broad appeal in the marketplace due, primarily, to the addition of a smart contract capability. However, you have to pay to use the Ethereum platform in the form of having to burn Ether for every line of code executed. But, no matter how you measure it, Ethereum is the most widely used Blockchain in the market.

HYPERLEDGER HyperLedger, with its blue chip project participants like IBM, Oracle, and Intel are looking to build industry vertical consortium's that use the Blockchains provided by the HyperLedger project. But, it is clear that some of these blue chip project participants have an ulterior motive in promoting their version of the HyperLedger Blockchain by pushing their related services and hardware along with the Blockchain technology.

c•rda Then there is Corda, which focused so much on the requirements of the banking and finance world, that instead of a blockchain distributed ledger, they ended up with a "shared ledger" platform where consensus on transactions is reached only between the parties involved in the transaction. However, Corda is able to operate in strict privacy in an open, distributed, global network.

Then you have Ripple, which focused on doing one thing well: building a Blockchain that met the criteria for a global payment platform. Ripple has achieved this by providing for fast, frictionless, global payments.

 The next evolution of Blockchain may well come from EOS whose goal is to become the first blockchain operating system to provide uniform system services to enable faster distributed application development. And, unlike Ethereum, EOS allows for free use of the system and will give the world the first "Blockchain-aware" operating system

This concludes Chapter 9 on the evolving blockchain. Chapter 10 will look at some sample applications and the future of Blockchain

CHAPTER 10
Sample Applications and the Future

Chapter 10 will list the circumstances that should be considered when trying to decide on using a Blockchain - or not - for a given application. Four sample application scenarios will be analyzed and contrasted, looking at a traditional approach to developing those applications on one hand and the alternative approach using Blockchain. Finally, some of the challenges ahead for Blockchain and what to look for in the future will be presented as part of the conclusion of this book.

Deciding on Blockchain – Evaluation Criteria

There are several considerations to make when trying to decide if Blockchain is the right platform for your application. The considerations that will be analyzed here are:

1. The network effect

2. Does the application need disintermediation?

3. Will the application benefit from tokenization?

4. What level of confidentiality does the data involved in the application need?

The Network Effect - The first criteria that must be met when considering using a Blockchain to build a distributed application is what I like to call the network effect. This is the idea that blockchains are only needed if there is a *network* of users or nodes participating in the application. The larger the network, the more powerful certain characteristics of the Blockchain become, like immutability and resistance to attacks. The more copies of the distributed ledger that are scattered across multiple nodes, the more difficult it is to hack the system. It is a difficult task to recruit a network for a Blockchain, especially for private Blockchains, where the needed participants exist *outside* of your company. Attempting to overcome the network effect is why you will see industry vertical consortiums being built to make sure the network is robust enough. According to a study conducted by Deloitte Consulting in August of 2017, there are over 40 global consortia across six different industries that have been formed in pursuit of blockchain solutions. Because, being the only node on a network for blockchain is like being the only person in the world with a phone…who are you going to call?

Disintermediation - The second criteria involves asking the question, "does your application need disintermediation?" Are third party verifiers used by this application and are you looking to eliminate those third parties? Blockchains enable multiple parties who do not fully trust each other to safely and directly share a single distributed ledger without requiring a trusted intermediary. Another indicator to check is whether or not multiple signatures are needed in the verification process of a transaction. A study conducted by IBM on international shipping showed that 17 signatures were required to move goods through a port for a shipment overseas. All of these signatures could potentially be eliminated with Blockchain.

Tokenization - The third consideration is the tokenization of assets and data. Tokenization of an asset is the idea of putting the rights to an asset into a digital token on a Blockchain. Does your application need to have assets tokenized?

Tokenization of data is slightly different from the tokenization of an asset in that tokenization of data is the process of replacing sensitive data with unique symbols that retain all the essential information *about* the data without exposing the data directly. The tokens supported by the value of the data are encapsulated within a block, and the original data could be encrypted or hashed or stored in a database outside the Blockchain.

Once an asset is represented by a token, the ownership, movement and provenance of the asset is more portable and sharable across the network. For example, healthcare providers will soon issue tokens that offer historical proof of care and the collective actions taken by the patient and provider. While these tokens will act as verification of the patient's health history, they will not reveal sensitive health details about the patient.

Confidentiality - The last consideration is confidentiality. Can your application tolerate the fact that all participants in a Blockchain see all the transactions that took place on that Blockchain? Even if advanced cryptography is used to hide some aspects of transactions, a Blockchain will always reveal more information than a centralized database due to the trustless nature of Blockchain. As you contemplate the purpose of your application, is it possible for *all* the participants in the network to share a single distributed ledger or are there corporate or security, or other reasons that would restrict this open sharing of the data? Also, is keeping all the history of an application all the time, a necessity? After a certain amount of time has elapsed, is there any value to having a complete history? Effectively, Blockchains represent a trade-off in which the elimination of trusted third parties is gained at the cost of confidentiality.

So, before deciding on whether or not Blockchain is the proper platform for your next application, make sure to consider these four issues.

Sample Application Scenarios

As we examine some application scenarios, we will first observe the application in a traditional processing environment and then look at the impact that adding a Blockchain might have on that same application scenario. Four application scenarios will be examined:

1. Financial Application
2. Provenance Tracking Application
3. Data Notary Application
4. Internet of Things and Blockchain

Sample Financial Application

Here we have two participants who want to do business together. They may want to transfer money, trade stocks, bonds or other financial instruments. To facilitate these transactions, a trusted third party like a broker or banker is needed. In his example, Participant E wants to transfer money to Participant A. Refer to Figure 96 below to follow the transaction flow.

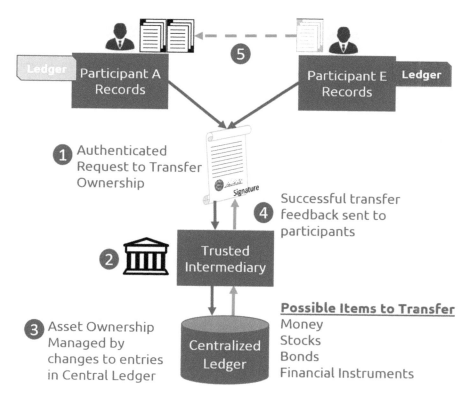

Figure 96 - Sample financial application flow

1. To start the transaction rolling, some type of authenticated request to transfer ownership must be mutually agreed upon between the parties. These could be paper documents or electronic forms, either of which would need some form of verified signature and, usually, some kind of third-party verification.

2. The authenticated request is sent to the trusted third-party who ensures that all the paperwork is in order. The trusted third-party will also ensure that the assets that are to be transferred are rightfully owned by the participant who is trading the asset and that the participant buying the asset has the wherewithal to purchase the asset.

3. Once the trusted third-party confirms that the transaction is valid, the asset ownership is adjusted by modifications made directly to a central database.

4. The feedback that the modifications have been made (shown by the solid red arrows in Figure 96) is sent back to the transacting parties and the assets are accordingly transferred.

5. Each participant adjusts their local ledger accordingly. Note in this example, both participants are using the same trusted third-party. It is not unusual for each participant to use separate ones.

Note that if a mistake is made and the asset was transferred in error, or in the wrong amount, these mistakes can quickly and easily be reversed through ledger entries made directly to the central database.

Traditional Financial Application Issues

This scenario seemed to work fine, so what are the issues? First, there is the time-consuming paper trail of filling out forms, authenticating signatures, and gaining counter signatures. Depending on the type of transaction, multiple documents may be involved.

Next is the issue with centralization of control. Having a single copy of the ledger in one place is a huge security risk from both inside and outside the company. This is a significant security challenge, in both technical and human terms. Inside the company, an employee could make changes to alter account values and this kind of attack is hard to detect. What is even worse is the negative impact this kind of misconduct has on the clients of the trusted third party. From outside the company, hackers have a single target where they can concentrate their efforts to breach the system. If the hackers are successful, they can change the ledger at will, stealing funds or destroying the ledger completely. And, it is expensive to maintain the integrity of the central ledger. In addition to the cost of security, both physical security and data security, there is the constant, ongoing verification and reconciliation between the centralized ledger and the transacting parties. If the ledgers ever get out of synch, it is a major problem.

Sample Financial Application with Blockchain

Now let's look at the same financial application scenario, but this time we will insert a Blockchain. Figure 97 shows the process flow and captures the pieces that are eliminated in the process.

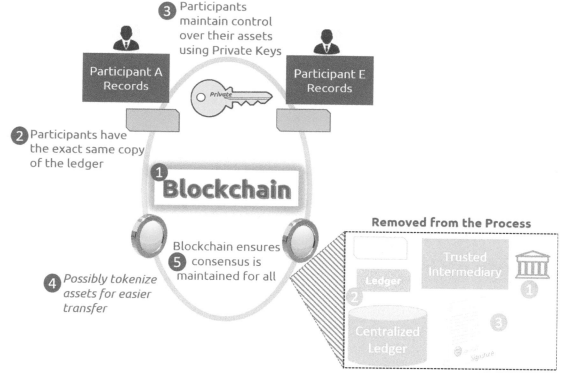

Figure 97 - Sample Financial Application using a Blockchain

1. The first thing that happens when the Blockchain is inserted is the trusted third-party is no longer needed.

2. Next, both the centralized ledger and the individual ledgers kept by the participants go away as all the participants now share the exact same copy of the distributed ledger.

3. Authenticated documents disappear as the participants will now use cryptographic keys for identification and authentication inside the Blockchain.

4. Further, assets can be tokenized to make it easier to transfer and transact with the asset inside the Blockchain.

5. The Blockchain itself ensures that the quantities and value of transactions is known and agreed upon by the participants through the use of a consensus algorithm.

Benefits of the Blockchain Approach

With Blockchain, there is no central point of attack since every participant will have their own duplicate copy of the ledger. Transactions propagate in a peer-to-peer fashion with a Blockchain, and the built-in consensus algorithm ensures that consensus that the ledger is automatically reconciled in real-time which saves time and money in the process.

So, what is the downside of using a Blockchain? Confidentiality. Since a Blockchain maintains a complete history of *all* transactions and every participant (there would, most likely, be more than two participants in a Blockchain network) has a copy of the distributed ledger, meaning that *any* of the participants can see *any* of the transactions on the Blockchain – whether or not that participant was involved in the transaction. If this notion is a problem, then forget using a Blockchain.

Other Possible Financial Applications

Having looked at a somewhat generic financial example to highlight the potential benefits of Blockchain, here is a list of possible financial applications that could certainly benefit from Blockchain:

- Currency exchange
- Payments & Remittance
- Clearing &Settlement
- Gift cards
- Loyalty Points
- Trading
- Crowdfunding
- Audit.

In the above cases, confidentiality tends to be less of an issue – even if the participants pay close attention to what each other are doing, they won't learn much of value. And, because the stakes are low, it is preferable to avoid the hassle and cost of setting up an intermediary.

The critical Blockchain properties that are being exploited in these applications are:

- Cryptographic Ledger
- Decentralized Network Control
- Trustless Counterparties
- Independent Consensus

The next example application we will review is provenance tracking.

Traditional Provenance Tracking Application

In this sample application, a manufacturer wants to be able to track the origin and movement of high-value items across a supply chain. Figure 98 below shows the application flow.

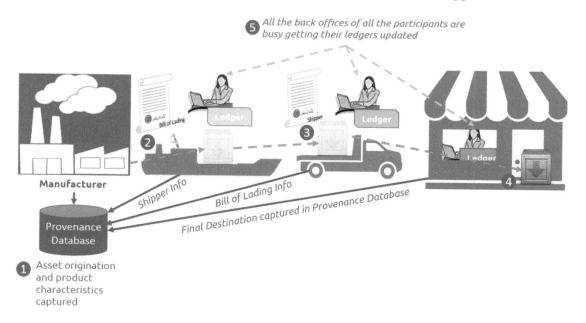

Figure 98 - Sample provenance tracking application flow

1. So, as goods are made, the asset origination and product characteristics are captured in the manufacturer's provenance database. The information captured would include serial number, weight, quality assurance data, among other information about that product.

2. Now the manufacturer wants to ship the product to a retailer and employs a shipping company to transport the goods. A bill of lading is filled out and signed off on as the product is loaded on to the ship. At some point, this bill of lading information would be updated in the manufacturer's provenance database. This update could be in real time or sometime after, depending on the application.

3. When the ship finally lands in port, the product now needs to be transferred to a truck to complete the overall shipment. Again, documentation in the form of a shipper must be signed off on and the associated information is captured in the manufacturer's provenance database.

4. Finally, the product makes it to the final destination of a retail store. The acceptance of the package and the condition of the product are noted, and the provenance database is again updated.

5. Meanwhile, in the background, the various back offices of the shipping company, the trucking company, and the retailer, are all busy updating their piece of the transaction into their own respective ledgers.

Traditional Provenance Tracking Issues

The first issue is the time-consuming paper trail. Bills of lading, shippers, and the final receipt to the retailer all must be signed off on and copies left behind as the transaction unfolds. Another issue is the asynchronous flow of information. Each of the participants in this transaction would receive the update data from the field at different times and, most likely, through different deliver mechanisms – some in real time and others as the paperwork flowed back to the main office. And, as was the case with the financial example, there are the two issues of concentration of control and the expense of maintaining the integrity of the central database - are also issues with this application. The same security and synchronization issues are present in the provenance tracking application with the same concerns as we uncovered with the sample financial application.

Sample Provenance Tracking using Blockchain

Refer to Figure 99 below to follow the process flow of the sample provenance tracking application using a Blockchain.

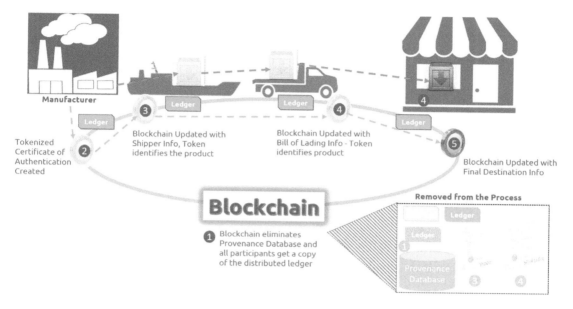

Figure 99 - Sample provenance tracking application flow using blockchain

1. Adding the blockchain eliminates the central provenance data base, and an exact copy of the data is distributed to all the participants in the supply chain. This also eliminates the extra accounting work that is performed by each of the participants.

2. When the product is manufactured, a tokenized "certificate of authenticity" is captured in the Blockchain to authenticate the product's point of origin. The token also helps address counterfeiting and theft which is a major problem with supply chains. A digitized token is far harder to steal or forge than a piece of paper. The movement of the token is shown by following the green, dashed arrows in Figure 99.

3. As the product starts its journey to the retailer, the shipping information is captured in the Blockchain and the certificate of authenticity correctly identifies the exact product. Since the bill of lading information has been stored in the Blockchain, the paper copy of the shipper is no longer needed. The product is loaded on the ship as shown by the red, dashed arrow in Figure 99, and the token is then transferred to the shipping company.

4. When the product is transferred to the truck, the bill of lading information is captured in the Blockchain and the certificate of authenticity is passed on to the trucking company to virtually mirror the physical transfer of the product. Since the bill of lading information has been stored in the Blockchain, its paper copy is no longer needed.

5. When the product reaches its final destination, the certificate of authenticity is checked one last time to make sure the real product was not swapped out and the retailer information is updated in the Blockchain. When the retailer accepts delivery of the product and transfer of the token, the retailer can verify the chain of custody for the product all the way back to the manufacturer. By tracking the digital token on the blockchain every time the product changed hands, the Blockchain precisely mirrors the real-world chain of custody through a chain of transactions on the Blockchain.

Benefits of the Blockchain Approach

The first benefit of using a Blockchain is that the paper trail of documents is completely eliminated. As the status of the shipment is captured in the Blockchain, the updates are authenticated through distributed consensus, so there is no need for paper documents. Since every participant in the supply chain shares the same copy of the distributed ledger, everyone is working off the same data at the same time, and each participant has to contribute their input to enable the product to reach its final destination. These updates are now equally available to all participants in near real-time. Effectively, the Blockchain forces the *trust* that the manufacturer had when the process began to be distributed among all the participants. Finally, the chain of custody and shipment status is readily available to all the participants and can be viewed in real-time or historically.

Possible Provenance Tracking Applications

Having looked a somewhat generic example to highlight the potential benefits of Blockchain, here is a list of possible provenance tracking applications that could benefit from Blockchain.

- Precious Metals
- Luxury Goods
- Electronics
- Component Parts
- Pharmaceuticals
- Quality Assurance

The critical Blockchain properties that are being exploited in these applications are:

- Cryptographic Ledger
- Decentralized Network
- Trustless Counterparties
- Immutability

Next, a data notary application scenario will be contrasted.

Sample Data Notary Application Scenario

Both of the previous sample applications were based on tokenized *assets*, which are *on-chain* representations of an item of value. Blockchain technology can also be used to protect *data* as well as assets. In this example, an audit trail of critical communications between three organizations in the legal sector is needed. Since none of the individual organizations in the group can be trusted with the archive of records, a trusted third-party is needed. Figure 100 shows the process flow of this type of application without using a Blockchain.

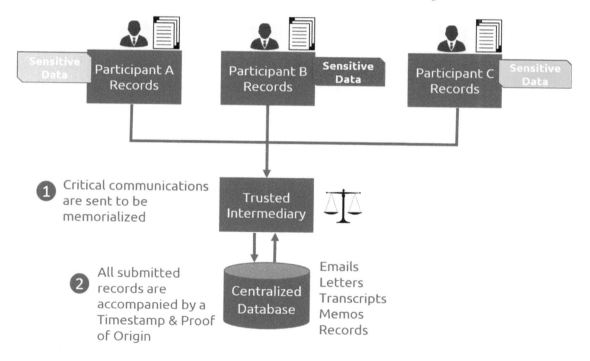

Figure 100 - Sample data notary application process flow

1. The participants each send their critical communications/information to a trusted intermediary to protect the integrity of the data.

2. The trusted third-party must set up a shared database into which all of the records are written, with each record accompanied by a timestamp and proof of origin. Examples of the type of information that might be collected are emails, letters, transcripts, memos, and other records of interest. In the end, it is vital that all participants agree on the archive's contents in order to prevent or settle disputes.

Traditional Data Notary Issues

Primarily, the concentration of control issue is the main concern along with the internal and external security issues for all the same reasons as were described earlier in the sample financial application. And, in this scenario, you also have the potential damage that might be caused to one or more of the participants if the data is wrongly falsified or deleted. Again, as we saw in the other application scenario examples, it is expensive to maintain the integrity of the central database. And, the issues of synchronization and data transfers just compounds as more participants, whose records need to be collected, are added.

Sample Data Notary application scenario with Blockchain

In the sample data notary application scenario, the Blockchain acts as a mechanism for collectively recording and notarizing any type of data. Figure 101 below shows the process flow and changes that are introduced when a blockchain is used in a data notary application:

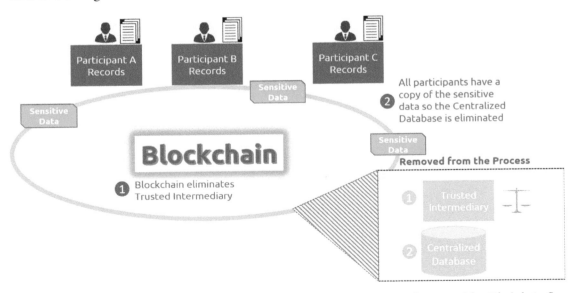

Figure 101 - Data notary application with a Blockchain flow

1. By introducing the Blockchain, the trusted intermediary can be eliminated.

2. Also, all the sensitive data is encapsulated in the Blockchain where all the participants will have their own, identical copy of the data, thereby eliminating the centralized database. Also, the immutability of Blockchain removes the possibility of anyone corrupting the data.

Data Options

How the data gets stored inside the blockchain can vary in three different ways. The first option is *unencrypted*. Figure 101 above is an accurate representation of what the application would look like with unencrypted data. Not encrypting the data means that every participant can read the data in the Blockchain. This option yields the most transparency and can result in faster resolution of disputes. However, this exposes every bit of information for everyone on the Blockchain to see.

Another option is to *encrypt the data*. Figure 102 below shows how the scenario changes if you add encryption to the data.

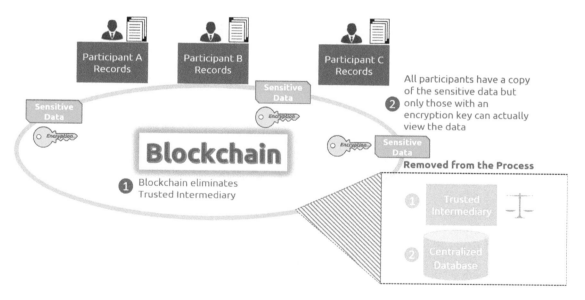

Figure 102 - Data notary application with encrypted data on a blockchain

Using the encryption option, the only participants that can read the data are those with the appropriate decryption key. This decryption key can be revealed to a trusted authority like a court, and the Blockchain can be used to prove that the original data was added by a specific party at a certain point in time to help settle a dispute.

The last option for how the data is internally stored on the Blockchain is to *hash the data.* Figure 103 below shows the subtle changes that would appear in the Application flow.

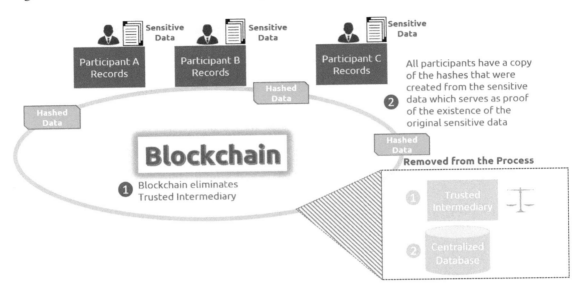

Figure 103 - Data notary application with hashed data on a Blockchain

As was discussed in Chapter 2, a hash acts as a *digital fingerprint* for the data that is input to the hash algorithm. Hashes also have the added benefit of always being represented in 32 bytes, regardless of the size of the text string that was input to the hash algorithm. The hash can be verified without having to reveal the data used to generate it. With the approach illustrated in Figure 103, the hash is placed on the Blockchain, with the original data stored *off-chain* by interested parties, who can reveal the source data in case of a dispute. If even one character of the sensitive data is changed while off-chain, and the data was brought forward to settle a dispute, the hash that would be generated when the sensitive data is hashed again would *not* match the original hash, signaling that the data was tampered with.

Benefits of Data Notary Application using a Blockchain

There is a huge savings on transferring and synching the data when the central database is replaced with a Blockchain. Digital signatures and consensus ensure the integrity of the data, regardless of what technique was used to store the data on the Blockchain. Also, the append-only nature of Blockchain ensures that the data cannot be tampered with after the fact. There is no *update* or *delete* command in Blockchain. Strong hashing can be used for data verification without revealing content of the data. Confidentiality is not an issue for the data in this scenario, because the entire purpose is to create a shared archive that all the participants can see when needed - even if some data is encrypted or hashed.

Possible Data Notary Applications

Having looked at a somewhat generic example to highlight the potential benefits of Blockchain, here is a specific list of possible data notary applications that could profit from blockchain

- Medical Records
- Security Camera Footage
- IP Documents
- Consortium Data Storage
- Chain of Custody for protecting evidence
- Courtroom Documents

The critical Blockchain properties that are being exploited in these applications are:

- Crypto-Ledger
- Decentralized Network
- Trustless Counterparties
- Immutability
- Append-only Data

Blockchain and the Internet of Things

According to Wikipedia, the Internet of things is the network of physical devices, vehicles, home appliances, and other items embedded with electronics, software, sensors, actuators, and network connectivity which enable these objects to connect and exchange data. The Internet of things has been touted as the *next big thing* in computing for the last several years. Of course, that was before the ***next*** *next big thing*, Blockchain, came along. This begs the question, "what would happen if the two *next big things* were combined in an application? What would be the impact? Figure 104 below shows a sample application flow of strawberries being shipped from the farm to their final destination in a grocery store.

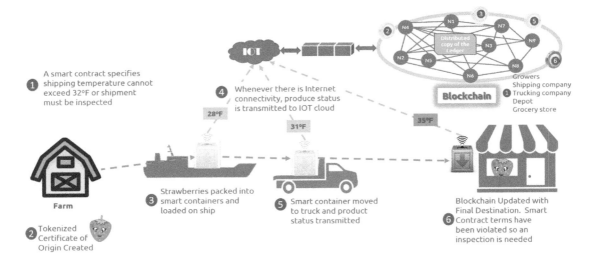

Figure 104 - IoT and Blockchain application flow

1. The first step is that all the participants in this scenario agree on the terms of a smart contract. In this example, the smart contract is focused only on the temperature of the containers that will hold the strawberries during the shipping process. The participants include the growers, shipping company, trucking company, depot and the grocery store. The container temperature cannot exceed 32° Fahrenheit or the container must be opened for inspection and possible rejection.

2. The origin of the strawberries is tokenized so as the shipment progresses, the various handlers of the produce can be assured that they have the correct produce and also report on the location of the shipment through the Blockchain.

3. The strawberries are loaded into smart containers. The smart containers are equipped with special BOLOS-core sensor devices that monitor the temperature of the container. In Chapter 8, the BOLOS-core sensors were detailed. These BOLOS-core sensors are Blockchain-aware and also have a private key for device identity and a special anti-tampering capability if the device comes under attack. The token is updated to show that the shipping company now has possession of the strawberries.

4. Because the smart containers are network capable, whenever there is connectivity to the Internet, the current status information of the produce is transmitted to the IoT cloud and then replicated in the distributed ledger across the blockchain. So far, the smart containers are reporting that the temperature is 28° Fahrenheit which is within the allowable temperature range specified in the smart contract.

5. The ship reaches the depot and the smart container is now transferred to the truck. Since there is Internet connectivity at the depot, the smart container transmits status information to the IoT cloud. The temperature is 31° Fahrenheit which is still within the allowable temperature range specified in the smart contract. The token is updated to show that the trucking company now has possession of the strawberries.

6. The smart container reaches its final destination at the grocery store. Since there is Internet connectivity there, the smart container transmits the latest produce status information. Now, the temperature being reported by the smart container is 35° Fahrenheit. The temperature is above the allowable container temperature that was detailed in the smart contract. Therefore, the container must be opened for a physical inspection before the produce will be accepted.

What Blockchain brings to IoT

The most significant benefits that blockchain brings to the Internet of things revolve around identity. Since the "things" referred to in the Internet of things are all types of electronic devices, it is paramount that the devices have an unchallengeable identity. This begins with capturing the relevant characteristics of the device, like serial number, manufacturer, firmware and anything else that is relevant. Each device is assigned a digital identity and digital signature in the form of a private key. Devices should be able to send "challenge" and "response" messages to ensure that the device is in control of its own identity. Tamper-proof characteristics as are available in BOLOS-core devices will ensure that devices are not compromised.

Over time, a "reputation history" will emerge for the devices – especially when the device has proven to be reliable. And, as we saw in the provenance application example scenario earlier, the Blockchain can ensure authenticity and origin, while providing the full provenance of all product or produce being shipped. This would provide for an auditable chain of custody record of the movements of an asset. Finally, combining a Blockchain with IoT unifies the process and methods of validation for all the participants in the process.

Instead of the shipping company, matching shippers with signatures and port stamps to verify the location of the shipment, while the grower must wait for confirmation through a back channel of paper document flow, the near real-time updates to the distributed ledger in the Blockchain gives *all* the participants in the process the same information that has been confirmed through the consensus method inside the Blockchain.

When you mix smart contracts, distributed shared ledgers, device identity, provenance of the movement of assets, immutability, and shared consensus of Blockchain with smart containers, intelligent sensors, and store and forward data capabilities of the Internet of Things, it is clear that ***two*** *Next Big Things* are better than one!

Challenges for Blockchain

There are several challenges facing Blockchain adoption, but the three biggest challenges are:

1. Uncertainty around regulations
2. The network effect
3. Lack of standards

Regulations - One of the biggest challenges for Blockchain is the uncertainty around regulations. This includes issues of jurisdiction and applicable law should something go wrong. By definition, Blockchains have no specific location and could have nodes all over the world. This potentially leaves each network node subject to different legal requirements. Determining liability also represents a concern, as there may be no individual party ultimately responsible for the functioning of a blockchain and associated information. There are similar concerns as it relates to smart contracts and financial instruments and currencies. This is an area which requires a lot of focus in the near future.

The Network Effect - Another concern is the network effect. In a public Blockchain, this is less of a concern as anyone can decide to participate in the network. For private Blockchains, this might be one of the biggest impediments to blockchain adoption. It is a difficult task to recruit a network for the Blockchain when the needed participants exist outside of your company. The success of the various industry consortiums like R3 in banking, B3I in the insurance industry and hashed health in the health industry are ensuring that enough participation of integral companies in each of these industry verticals participates to make the Blockchain useful. Without a robust network, Blockchain is not as effective. Or, said another way, the more network nodes, the more powerful the Blockchain.

Standards - Finally, another challenge for Blockchain is the lack of standards. In some ways, this is driving innovation as vendors bring their version of different Blockchain features and functions to the market. But, how many consensus methods are really needed? Is there one, best way to run a smart contract? How many programming and scripting languages are needed to code functional extensions to Blockchain? So, while blockchain is an exciting technology, challenges remain.

Blockchain Is Not for Everything

I trust by now, you have a clear idea of what a blockchain *is* and what it *isn't*. As powerful as Blockchain technology is, it is not for everything. For example, Blockchain is *not* suited for high volume transactions that need millisecond response time. As we saw in Chapter 9, the highest transaction throughput of any existing Blockchain is 1,500 transactions per second from Ripple. EOS, if it lives up to its promise, may surpass that level, but high-volume transaction type of applications are not well suited for Blockchain. You also don't need a Blockchain for applications that do not require other companies or participants in a network. Blockchain is for *distributed* applications and the larger the network, the more secure, the application. If your application is entirely internal, then a Blockchain is not needed. Blockchains are not suitable as a random-access database. Since there is no indexing scheme in blockchain, then applications that require multiple indexes and views of the data would not be a good fit for Blockchain. Before deciding on blockchain to build your application, be sure the evaluate the criteria that was discussed earlier in this chapter.

Conclusion

There is no question that Blockchain is the *Next Big Thing* in computing. It promises to significantly reduce, streamline, or eliminate certain back office functions yielding huge potential savings to corporations and governments. Trusted third-parties and other intermediaries can be eliminated through the network consensus methods of Blockchain. A full history is automatically kept as a normal function of blockchain. Through the use of advanced cryptography and digital identities, Blockchain is immutable. Blockchain resist changes once data is stored and the further back in the Blockchain and the larger the network, the more difficult it is to make changes.

But, there are still many challenges left for the Blockchain world. The uncertainty around regulations and compliance is a big concern. The network effect can keep potential

Blockchain projects from ever getting off the drawing board. Will all the participants needed for the Blockchain to be effective, choose to participate? Lack of standards in several areas like consensus, smart contracts, scripting languages, block size, etc. make understanding Blockchains confusing. This leaves organizations with the warm and fuzzy feeling that the investment they are making in one of the many current approaches to Blockchain might end up the way of Betamax recorders. They work, but you are on the outside looking in as another approach becomes the standard for a whole industry. When stronger standards are agreed upon, this will only increase the adoption rate of Blockchain. Finally, Blockchain needs to be better understood in terms of what it can and what it cannot do which will ultimately lead to broader acceptance. Hopefully, this book helped *you* with your understanding of Blockchain.